# MACDIARMID

## AN ILLUSTRATED BIOGRAPHY

# MACDIARMID

## AN ILLUSTRATED BIOGRAPHY
### of
### Christopher Murray Grieve
### (Hugh MacDiarmid)
### by
### Gordon Wright

GORDON WRIGHT PUBLISHING
55 MARCHMONT ROAD, EDINBURGH, EH9 1HT
SCOTLAND

S.B.N. 903065 17 7


Published with the financial assistance of
the Scottish Arts Council

Printed in Scotland by Lindsay & Co. Ltd., 17 Blackfriars Street,
Edinburgh EH1 1ND

# CONTENTS

PUBLISHED IN 1977 TO CELEBRATE
THE EIGHTY-FIFTH BIRTHDAY OF
CHRISTOPHER MURRAY GRIEVE (HUGH MACDIARMID)
11TH AUGUST 1977

# PREFACE

I first met Hugh MacDiarmid in October 1967 when I visited his home to photograph him for *Catalyst* magazine. Since then, I have photographed him on several other occasions and over the years we have become friends. The idea to produce and publish an illustrated account of MacDiarmid's life was conceived in the spring of 1974. A London publisher had just issued a short, illustrated biography of a prominent literary figure and when I had a chance to examine a copy of the book, I was immediately inspired to produce a more extensive work on MacDiarmid.

In June 1974 I arranged to visit MacDiarmid at his home, outlined my proposal, and asked if he would be prepared to co-operate. I had briefly described what production would entail, I was prepared to research and compile all the material necessary to produce the book if he would help to identify photographs, allow me as many interviews as required and in the summer, accompany me to his native Langholm for a photo session which would be more of a pleasure jaunt than a chore. MacDiarmid agreed.

In the autumn of 1974, free from other publishing commitments and able to make a start, I visited MacDiarmid at his home again, and we started to sift through the considerable number of photographs Mrs Grieve had carefully collected over the years. As photographs were selected, they were labelled with as much information as possible, inserted in a protective plastic sleeve and filed in a loose-leaf folder in chronological order. From this skeleton the book evolved.

I then produced a large-format diary covering the eighty-two years of MacDiarmid's life and started to collate facts about his activities during the period. I circulated as many of his acquaintances as I could find, inviting them to contact me if they could offer any illustrative material for reproduction. Those who were kind enough to reply often suggested other possibilities and so the circle widened and more material was gathered.

During my months of research I contacted forty-seven newspapers and photographic agencies and was able to trace several items of great value, all accurately detailed and dated, the most important factor in piecing such a story together. Whenever possible, I visited the people who had responded to my enquiries and usually found that more information would be recalled during the conversation, filling in gaps and extending other pieces.

Originally it was intended merely to link illustrative material with captions to form a picture of MacDiarmid's life and achievements. However, as work progressed, it became impossible to ignore the many interesting facts that came to light, so like Topsy, the book just growed.

MacDiarmid has often amazed me by reminiscing in great detail, but the many highlights in such a long and distinguished career are difficult to date accurately without the diary he never kept. So it became necessary to cross-check dates, facts and figures with as many sources of information as possible, and by linking Press coverage, dated correspondence, travelling schedules, public events, celebrations, and publication dates of his books and magazines, I was able to retrace his steps with reasonable accuracy. So the book was researched and produced, and the publication of 144 pages planned in 1974 was eventually expanded to 176 pages by the time it reached the printer three years later.

To those who are only familiar with MacDiarmid as poet and leader of the modern Scottish Literary Renaissance, this book will reveal the many other sides of the man. Most important of these were his social and political involvements. Whether at community level as an Independent Socialist councillor, parish councillor, Justice of the Peace, member of the School Management Committee or as Nationalist or Communist candidate for parliamentary election, he always led the demonstration, was always controversial, always attracting attention for his cause with his pen and his formidable oratory. Is there anyone in Scotland today capable of filling the same breach?

Recognition has been slow in coming to Hugh MacDiarmid but now it is coming in good measure from many parts of the world. Just because he is so much of an elder statesman, just because he has done so much, it is not always easy to remember the debt Scotland owes him. Perhaps this record will impress on Scots and non-Scots alike something of the richness and diversity of his life spent fighting for his vision of a new Scotland.

Undoubtedly one of the most enjoyable parts of producing this book was the many new friends I made *en route*. These people were mostly from the world of the Arts, and interviewing them became an education in itself.

If any details are known to be incorrect, I would be pleased to be informed. If another edition is called for, a little rearrangement may be made and a little polish added.

Throughout this book Christopher Murray Grieve and his pseudonym Hugh MacDiarmid are referred to as C.M.G. to avoid confusion.

Special thanks are due to:

Dr and Mrs Grieve for their patience and kindness in allowing me access to their personal collection of photographs and Press cuttings and recalling in detail the many events in their life together;
Mr Walter Grieve and Mrs Alastair MacIntosh, C.M.G.'s first son and daughter, for confirming certain family events in the 1930s;
Mr Michael Grieve, C.M.G.'s second son, for reading the manuscript and helping to locate material;
Miss Jean White, C.M.G.'s cousin, for confirming early family details;
Dr Kenneth Buthlay, for writing the Introduction;
Dr W. R. Aitken, for supplying a selection of material for consideration, making many helpful suggestions, researching several important details and approving the finished manuscript;
Dr Ian Campbell, for reading the finished manuscript, confirming certain details and making many helpful suggestions;
Mr J. K. Annand, for undertaking research in the archives of Broughton School, supplying details and copy from his own private collection of papers and reading the finished manuscript;
Mr Ronald Stevenson, who acted as my adviser on musical affairs providing valuable detail on the work of Kaikhosru Shapurji Sorabji and Francis George Scott;
Mr Kulgin Duval and Mr Colin Hamilton, for supplying material from their own private collection and information on the work of Dr Mardersteig;
Mr Duncan Glen, who kindly supplied a selection of pamphlets and photographs and whose own publications were a valuable source of information;
Mr Norman MacCaig, for reading the finished manuscript;
Mr Michael Donnelly, The People's Palace Museum, Glasgow, for supplying a selection of material for reproduction;
Mr Stanley Simpson, Mr Max Begg and the staff of the National Library of Scotland;
Mr Charles Finlayson, Keeper of Manuscripts, Edinburgh University Library;
The staff of the Scottish Room, Edinburgh Central Library;
The staff of the Mitchell Library, Glasgow;
and finally, to the many people who were good enough to speak to me by phone, and the one hundred and thirty-seven who were kind enough to meet me, recall their reminiscences of C.M.G. and supply items for consideration.

Without their help this book would never have been completed.

Gordon Wright
Edinburgh, 1977

# HUGH MACDIARMID: WHERE EXTREMES MEET

## by Kenneth Buthlay

Over twenty years ago there was a radio talk on the B.B.C. entitled "The Deterioration of the Scottish Face". The speaker was already familiar with those splendid old photographs by Octavius Hill which most of us have just recently caught up with, and he said he had been talking to two of the finest portrait photographers in Scotland who

> both lamented the appalling dearth of faces really worth photographing. . . . And they agreed with me at once when I said that it was only necessary to riffle through the wonderful studies of Scots men and women taken by an early photographer like Dr Octavius Hill to see how terrible the process of degeneration in the interval had been — how all the qualities of moral strength, experience of life, high intelligence, strong purpose, good judgment, individual character, force and dignity had been eliminated in the course of the past century from the faces of nearly all our people. . . . Even where an occasional Scot today has a similarity of face to some well-known type of Scottish face of the past, it is, alas, only with the similarity between an electric bulb that is off and one that is on.

But the speaker maintained that it is not necessary to go to Hill for evidence, since "almost any old family photograph album will serve the same purpose. Look through one, and deny if you can that the vast majority of faces today are very mean and empty, cheap-looking and inane, in comparison with the doughty visages of our grandparents and great-grandparents. The difference is as the difference between lions and mice". He was ready to concede that "the outer expression may be in itself relatively unimportant, but what it is the outer expression of cannot be dismissed so lightly, and a great increase in shallow empty faces is, I believe, a sure index to a yawning void in the very heart of our national existence".

The speaker was Hugh MacDiarmid, and one can judge from the photographs of him (or rather of his only begetter, Christopher Grieve) collected in this book to what extent he may be exempted from his own restrictions on contemporary Scottish physiognomy. He has said that he resembles his paternal grandfather facially ("a big brow and all the features squeezed into the lower half of my face"), and is so far from sharing the lack of physical distinction he complains of in his contemporaries that, from his teens onwards, he has found people turning round and gaping at him as he passed them in the street. "I have been told that this is due to my eyes," he says, "but I cannot see that there is anything unusual about my eyes — no insane glitter or anything of that sort — or about my expression, gait or anything else. Certainly it is not my hair; I used to have a head of towsy hair of the colour of teased rope, but it is not nearly so wild nowadays, and in any case it was never sufficiently unusual to explain the effect I am describing. (My only really unusual feature — too small, however to be noticed except under close scrutiny — are two holes, like piercings for earrings, at the upper ends of the joinings of my ears to my head. They are, of course, vestigial bracts — deriving from the gills of the fish-stage of our evolution)".

Maybe this is because, as he says elsewhere:

> I was sae used to waters as a loon
> That I'm amphibious still. A perfect maze
> O' waters is aboot the Muckle Toon,
> Apairt frae't often seemin' through the weather
> That sea and sky swap places a'thegither.

And indeed he had a special empathy for the Waterside folk of his birthplace, Langholm, especially in times of spate, when they "lived in their doors or windas as gin their hooses had nae insides. They could dae naething but look, or raither be lookit at, through and through, for it was the water that did the lookin' and no' them. There was nae question o' thinkin'. It was faur owre quick and noisy for that. It fair deaved them, and every noo

9

and then a muckle wave louped in through their een and swirled in their toom harnpans and oot again. That's what I mean when I say that the Waterside folk were brainless craturs. Brains were nae use there. To dae onything ava they'd to use something faur quicker than thocht — something as auld as the water itsel'. And thocht's a dryland thing and a gey recent yin at that."

My own acquaintance with him has stopped short of familiarity with his vestigial bracts, but I have observed with interest another part of his anatomy: his hands. These do not appear to be webbed, but they are sufficiently remarkable for me to have asked, as my one request regarding the other contents of this book, that they be given a place there. I trust this will not lead to my being associated with the young man who approached James Joyce in Zurich, begging to be allowed to kiss the hand that wrote *Ulysses*. "No," said Joyce. "It did lots of other things too."

In MacDiarmid's case the hands with their curiously flexible fingers do seem to me a living reminder of the artist who has survived, improbably enough, the rucks and mauls of his other personae:

> Like when Uncle Dick wi' his pinkie crookt
>     Made yon gesture o' his,
> A raither slow line, half-blocked, half-reprovin'
>     And suddenly Liz
>     — Dirty Dick! Liz Quiz! —
> In a slightly buoyant anapaestic tone
>     Threw the dog a bone,
> An' a wealth o' new rhythms was syne let loose
> To mither's dismay, a' through the hoose.

Others have noticed the hands, of course, though it is the head that always looms largest, as no doubt it should, in the view of a man whose life (despite the influence of the allegedly brainless Waterside folk) has been dedicated to the proposition that it is impossible to be over-intellectual.

> I remember him best as he used to sit, sagged back in front of his fireplace, his legs plaited together and curled beneath his armchair, one hand, the left, lying indolently beside him while the right one gripped his black pipe. Then he would bend down forwards to tap out ash on the hearth and, as he did so, his head would turn sideways towards where I sat. That head looked huge. The hair curled up from it like the grey-brown smoke of a volcano and, though his expression betrayed no more than a quick slant of curiosity, the force of the man became apparent. The features were small and squeezed into the lower half of the face, the brow high and myriad wrinkled, the nose a sharp jut forwards, the eyes sunk in deep sockets as though eroded by a surfeit of sight; the whole composition denied his posture of repose. Then, at last, when he rose and walked across the room with that swift jerky gait of his, talking all the while, as though keeping time to his footsteps, in a learned staccato, one would glimpse the vigour that had written his twenty-odd books and his millions of words of invective.

So wrote Burns Singer in 1957: the number of books requires considerable adjustment today, as a glance at his bibliography will show. Going further back, to 1934, and losing the myriad wrinkles in the process, there is a description by Eric Linklater, in his novel *Magnus Merriman,* of a character called Hugh Skene who seems rather familiar: "He had a smooth white face, dwarfed by a great bush of hair, and in brisk, delicate, rather terrier-like features his eyes shone bright and steady. His hands were beautifully shaped and somewhat dirty. . . . As if it were a pistol he aimed his slender and rather dirty forefinger at Magnus and said, with cold and deliberate ferocity: "You're feeding on corpse meat. In all its traditional forms English literature is dead, and to depend on the past for inspiration is a necrophagous perversion. We've got to start again, and the great literary problem confronting us today is to discover how far we must retract the horizontal before erecting a perpendicular.' "

"That's me to a T," said MacDiarmid of this description, and he added: "The dirty hands are, of course, due to my going with my hands constantly in pockets full of loose black tobacco." Of course! That little phrase, unremarkable enough here, is worth noticing. There are times when his over-use of it, particularly when writing about himself, becomes so compulsive that one begins to think of it as not merely a cheville, or verbal plug, but as a significant psychological tic, of serious interest to students of his character. Why should he feel the need to assure us so often that we can, "of course", take so much for granted about him?

But his is hardly the sort of character one would hope to analyse with a little amateur psychology. As the Drunk Man said of the Thistle, in MacDiarmid's greatest work, it embraces a routh of contraries, whose proliferation he has deliberately encouraged in himself, on the grounds that this is in accordance with the veridical Scottish ethos — the celebrated Caledonian Antisyzygy. According to this line of thought, your true Scot doesn't merely entertain conflicting ideas, he sets up house with them for life — lives with his Anti, you might say, if you were rash enough.

As a relatively simple example of the principle in operation — those who know the kindness, courtesy and generosity of Christopher Grieve, and the unfalse modesty with which he will talk about his own work, have simultaneously to come to terms with the man who declares: "I have no love for humanity, but only for the higher brain-centres— the human mind in which only a moiety of mankind has ever had, or has today, any part or parcel whatever. An intellectual snob of the worst description, in fact!" His kindness in the flesh is matched by his ferocity in print, an instance of which is memorably recorded by Leslie Mitchell (Lewis Grassic Gibbon) as follows:

> Several years ago I sat at tea with a pleasant Scottish lady who had just written a pleasant book of Scottish verse. She was showing me a sheaf of reviews — laudatory reviews, patronising reviews, deprecatory reviews. But only one had stirred her to any extent. . . . "The bloody little beast!" she remarked succinctly.
>
> It was C.M.G. Where other reviewers shambled on broken-knee'd jades, here was one who galloped on a warhorse. Dr J. M. Bulloch had written a preface to the book, and had sneered at synthetic Scots in the process, but not unchallenged. Having demolished the verse and its author in a few brief sentences, dishonoured the corpse, and stamped on its face, Grieve had caught up a battle-axe and chased the unfortunate Bulloch (that decent couthy body, who never wrote an offensive or intelligent thing in his life) down half a column of such magnificent invective as made your toes tingle. Then, wiping the blood from the blade, he came back, glanced at the verse, saw a flicker of life in it, extinguished it, and departed — probably to teach revolutionary tactics to Trotsky or confer with the leaders of the Pan-Negro Congress.

Mitchell noted that, paradoxically, MacDiarmid's "weakness in prose is his delight in word manipulation; he might refer to an adversary as a negligible person; instead, he refers to him as, say, a 'negligible, nefarious, knock-knee'd nonentity'. Like bringing up the tumbrils and guillotine to execute a rat". Or killing squirrels with a howitzer, as someone else has suggested. The criticism is a fair one, and indeed there is no denying that in his work as a whole, whether signing himself Grieve or MacDiarmid, he has always been a compulsive writer, subject to prolonged bouts of verbal intoxication. Still, most readers will be willing to put up with a good many failings for the sake of a few passages like this: "My aim all along has been (in Ezra Pound's term) the most drastic *desuetization* of Scottish life and letters, and, in particular, the de-Tibetanization of the Highlands and Islands, and getting rid of the whole gang of high mucky-mucks, famous fatheads, old wives of both sexes, stuffed shirts, hollow men with headpieces stuffed with straw, bird-wits, lookers-under-beds, trained seals, creeping Jesuses, Scots Wha Ha'evers, village idiots, policemen, leaders of white-mouse factions and noted connoisseurs of bread and butter, glorified gangsters, and what "Billy" Phelps calls Medlar Novelists (the medlar being a fruit that becomes rotten before it is ripe), Commercial Calvinists, makers of 'noises like a turnip', and all the touts and toadies and lickspittles of the English Ascendancy, and their infernal womenfolk, and all their skunkoil skulduggery.''

A compulsive writer, then, of overwhelming vitality, whose business in life, he says, has been "to secure a psychological revolution in Scotland". Compton Mackenzie called him "the most powerful intellectually and emotionally fertilising force Scotland has known since the death of Burns", and this seminal influence has penetrated to innumerable people who would consciously reject his ideas and deny his importance. His many books are only the tip of the iceberg. Since his return to Scotland from the first world war till what is now his eighty-fifth year, he has carried on a one-man propaganda movement aimed at shocking his countrymen out of their national sleep and coming at them from all directions — in heterogeneous material supplied to local newspapers, in signed journalism on a vast scale, in letters to editors, in talks, readings, speeches, lectures, television appearances, and in public controversies of all kinds. And, on the non-public side he has made himself perpetually available, with the greatest kindness and patience, to almost anyone who has cared to approach him.

The intensity of his preoccupation, not to say obsession, with Scotland is combined with a very wide range of reference, which he has laboured strenuously to expand throughout his career. This is one of the main reasons for the great variety of his work, which, at the cost of conspicuous unevenness, has earned him the right to boast of the faculty that attracts to him "all the available information on points no matter how obscure or technical from sources no matter how far scattered". When operating at peak efficiency, it "grangerizes" the issue that presently concerns him with "a simultaneous recollection of all manner of connected (or, no matter how remotely, connectable) matters", drawn from his omnivorous reading, and produces a "compenetrant complexity of relationships and ideas for their literary and political utilisation".

His verbal range is no less formidable, and in this connection his imaginative exploration of the Lowland Scots language indicates only one of the directions in which he strove to extend the linguistic frontiers of his poetry, though many would say it has proved the most rewarding. The service he did his native tongue by writing much of his finest poetry in it, and through it, is beyond computation; and a growing awareness of the language, however neglected or indeed rejected it has been in the course of our prolonged Anglicisation, is now a potent influence in the ambience of contemporary Scotland.

MacDiarmid's writing at all levels has played a vital part in stimulating a fresh interest in Scottish literature, for so long disposed of largely by paying lip-service to wee effigies of Robert Burns. His attacks on devotees of the Burns cult, and to some extent on Burns himself ("that Longfellow in all but leid" who he says was lacking in intellectual equipment), have destroyed much mindless complacency and illiterate Scottish bardolatry. Burns in the long run has benefited from a more critical awareness of his strengths and weaknesses, more serious thinking about his relation to predecessors such as Robert Fergusson and about the nature of his achievement and influence. Also, although MacDiarmid's methods and manner of approach were hardly likely to persuade Burns Club dignitaries to put it into practice, his vision of what the international Burns movement could become was admirably clear and far-sighted: a world-wide organisation whose Scottish interests would concentrate on Burns's "essential motives applied to crucial contemporary issues as he applied them while he was living to the crucial issues of his own time and generation. What a true Scottish Internationale that would be — what a culmination and crown of Scotland's rôle in history!"

Scotland's rôle in history, which for so many of his countrymen, if it ever existed, ceased to do so centuries ago, assumed for MacDiarmid the dimensions of myth, a "dynamic myth", a great creative idea. And it mattered little to him if its conception were to prove as far-fetched as Dostoevski's *Russian Idea* in the light of subsequent developments in Soviet Russia. His Scotland is a country of the mind,

> . . . the land I have dreamt of where the supreme values
> Which the people recognise are states of mind,
> Their ruling passion the attainment of higher consciousness.

And the particular mind in question, being MacDiarmid's, is forever being stretched to accommodate new influxes of information, of linguistic resources, and of speculative thought. To follow its flexions is at least good intellectual exercise: "jujitsu for the educated".

MacDiarmid says that, like Dostoevski, he will "aye be whaur extremes meet". What he values above all in his national inheritance are the "extraordinary contradictions of character, most dangerous antimonies and antithetical impulses" which he sees as "the incredible psychological background to the almost uniformly dull and commonsensical collection of appalling buddies that constitutes our Anglicised Scottish nation today". And he maintains that

> the essential point is that all fixed opinions — all ideas that are not entertained just provisionally and experimentally — every attempt to regard any view as permanent — every identification of Scottish genius with any particular religion or political doctrine — every denial of the relativity and transience of all thought, any failure to "play with" ideas — and above all the stupid (since self-stultifying) idea that ideas are not of prime consequence in their qualitative ratio and that it is possible to be over-intellectual — are anti-Scottish — opposed to our national genius, which is capable of countless manifestations at absolute variance with each other, yet confined within the "limited infinity" of the adjective "Scottish".

It's small wonder that a man who declares that what Scotland needs is "a great upwelling of the incalculable" should have been the despair of generations of practical politicians; nevertheless his contribution to the impetus of Scottish nationalism which has at last got through the condescension of Westminster *is* incalculable. He has seen himself as that unprepossessing creature the catfish, whose function is to vitalise "the other torpid denizens of the aquarium", and his success in this respect is essentially unaffected by whether his fellow Scots are aroused to acclamation or to denunciation, just so long as they as Scotsmen have been jolted out of their long apathy:

Wrang-heidit? Mm. *But heidit! That's the thing.*

Among the "dangerous antimonies" of the Scottish past there is one at least which he has denounced as falsely divisive, and has worked persistently to transcend: the dichotomy between Highland and Lowland. His ideas about the Celtic ethos of Scotland have been pushed in characteristic fashion to the extreme, culminating in a mythology of his own making which may seem at times as remote as Blake's. But along the way he has done a great deal towards fostering among Lowlanders an awareness of, and respect for, the Gaelic inheritance. He has given some of us at least a sufficiently bad conscience to set about acquiring some knowledge of Gaelic literature, and his influence on contemporary Gaelic writers themselves has encouraged them to see that that literature continues to live and develop. His versions of poems by Alexander MacDonald and Duncan Ban MacIntyre, made with the assistance of the outstanding contemporary Gaelic poet, Sorley MacLean, have stimulated interest in a wider readership through their inclusion in his anthology of Scottish poetry, the *Golden Treasury*; and much of his own work has been created within a Gaelic context.

I have mentioned his assaults on the old-style Burnsians. His directive to Scots poetry was away from Burns and back to Dunbar, essentially because Dunbar had the equipment and the cultural poise to write as a good European, and indeed the ability to make a contribution to the broad European tradition far beyond the reach of his English contemporaries. MacDiarmid hoped that an informed appreciation of the stature of Scots literature in Dunbar's day would stimulate a renewed sense of the European tradition among Scottish writers of our time, instead of what he condemned as a narrow preoccupation with English literature, which had itself become insular where not imperialist in outlook. So much for his "narrow nationalism" — and the more recent bogey of "separatism".

Part of MacDiarmid's brief has always been to keep himself and his readers informed of developments in European and ideally in world literature, with his Celtic interests serving as a meeting point for East and West. No doubt he exaggerated his own accomplishments in this as in other respects, but it is equally beyond doubt that he did know a great deal and has succeeded in stimulating many readers as he intended. How many have first got interested in — for example, among many Russian writers — Blok and Pasternak because of MacDiarmid's pioneering advocacy of these authors? The value of his versions of modern poets from various countries — whatever the cribs he used as intermediaries — is plain enough for those with eyes to see. And any reader who has followed up his leads into the less familiar territories of some foreign literatures will have enjoyed some lively and illuminating experiences.

His openness to a whole world of literature, of ideas, and (to an unusual extent for a poet) of science, was not occluded by his early decision to identify his interests with those of his own small country, which he did with such total commitment that by 1934 William Soutar was saying that the younger Scottish writers already saw him as a national symbol: "We begin to look back at him as we read: already he is becoming a symbol. . . . Within the chaos of post-war Europe has it not been a spiritual necessity, conscious or unconscious, which has driven so many minds down to their national roots: having no longer sufficient faith in a creed or a philosophy they seek to link their destiny with a nation's, and by a kind of self-sacrificing dedication find an equivalent for religious service. Nor can the gospel of these patriots be other than a voice from the wilderness; a John Baptist call to repentance; so that, in the poet, his poetry is at once condemnation and a cry for regeneration. Scotland, in the person of Hugh MacDiarmid, has such a poet. Since Burns there has been no manifestation of our national spirit comparable to MacDiarmid: and not only of our national spirit, but of the contemporary European psyche."

Elsewhere, Soutar went on to suggest, by reference to the dual rôles of Christopher Grieve and Hugh MacDiarmid, the completion of the biblical parallel:

> Renaissance was his challance an' his sang;
> An' at a' oors he dinn'd aboot the dird o't:
> But sin he was John Baptist far owre lang
> Wha'll blame him gin he's made himsell the Lord o't.

And it is true that MacDiarmid's *Drunk Man* saw himself as crucified on the *Thistle*, declaring:

> Aye, this is Calvary — to bear
> Your Cross wi'in you frae the seed,
> And feel it grow by slow degrees
> Until it rends your flesh apairt,
> And turn, and see your fellow-men
> In similar case but sufferin' less
> Thro' bein' mair wudden frae the stert!

This has been followed by someone remarking that he too was a man of sorrows and acquainted with Grieve. But Chris, we may be sure, will never be Christ to a T. "A God in Murray tartan" — his own description — maybe.

His experiences at certain periods of his life must have been enough to embitter any man, and he did not come through them unscathed, although having come through, he may be inclined to make light of them now. But one factor which seems to me unduly neglected in accounts of the man and his work is his daft — but really daft — sense of humour, which has survived all the bitterness, and but for which indeed one might doubt if he himself could have survived:

> Let's make a better joke in politics and art
> Than the English yet — and damn consistency!

This, from a writer so passionately committed to his ideas in politics and art, may be disconcerting, but it is worth more attention than it has been given if one wants to understand "the enormities", as he has said, "the enormities of which 'highbrows' of my type are capable — even in Scotland".

When he was a small boy, his headmaster warned his father about "the terrible vein of recklessness" in a child who was "so utterly unamenable to discipline of any kind, not in any overt acts of challenge or defiance, but behind his deceptively quiet exterior, inside himself — in the innermost recesses of his nature". The headmaster was right; and one can well understand the many subsequent admonitions delivered in headmasterly fashion to this *enfant terrible* up to and into his eighty-fifth year. But it is a solemn absurdity to indulge in too much head-shaking over the recklessness of a person who has been a self-declared extremist on principle all his life. Just as society needs its scapegoats, it needs its perpetual rebels, prepared to devote their lives to the principle that "we must oppose every attempt at finality — every system that seeks to constitute a closed order — every theory which threatens to put an end to the restless spirit of mankind; and as Dostoevski pointed out long ago, every human organisation sooner or later aims at that".

The time to worry about MacDiarmid is when he does appear to conform, as has seemed to happen on occasions when his Scots Puritan inheritance has answered all too promptly to the austere call of Marxism. Still, I suppose, if his principle that everything changes is true, then that principle must itself change and produce a stasis. In any case the MacDiarmid whose dialectic has sometimes stalled on the dogma of a political creed is still on more than speaking terms with the MacDiarmid who remarked:

> . . . I am like Zamyatin. I must be a Bolshevik
> Before the Revolution, but I'll cease to be one quick
> When Communism comes to rule the roost.

Whatever else he is, he can fairly claim with Whitman, "I am large, I contain multitudes." Operating on such a scale involves commensurate risks, and his failures are liable to be as spectacular as his successes. Equally, when he loses the place, massive search operations have to be launched before he can hope to find it again. The equipment he has amassed over the years is formidable, and he has often eked it out with brilliant improvisation, but, as a perpetual extremist, he has inevitably asked too much of it. This has resulted in his doing more than his share of wishful thinking, and although wishful thinking, no doubt, has been the beginning of a lot of art, it is only the beginning.

He has, however, admitted that he is not perfect on a number of occasions when the modest private man has persuaded the tub-thumping public figure to acknowledge his faults as well as his virtues. Of his overall contribution to Scottish literature he has said: "My job, as I see it, has never been to lay a tit's egg, but to erupt like a volcano, emitting not only flame but a lot of rubbish." It's true, his immense facility can be a menace to himself and to others. By rushing his worst productions into print with as much alacrity as his best, apparently applying the principle of "aye being where extremes meet" to matters of *quality*, he could not be other than vulnerable on a grand scale.

As early as 1930, in an anonymous review which he wrote of his book, *To Circumjack Cencrastus,* he deplored his own over-indulgence in needless personalities, gratuitious ill-will, pretentious pedantry, cheap sarcasm, and intellectual arrogance. In his *apologia, Lucky Poet,* he returned to the case against himself, saying: "My defects come partly from the nature of the tasks I set myself. I try to cover too much ground, repeat myself a lot, am often inconsistent, and not infrequently so dogmatic that one who really agrees with me feels nevertheless the temptation to ask, 'How do you know?'." But I suspect that the passage from which that is taken is itself a small example of a major weakness which he does not, however, mention: his massive over-indulgence in quotation, acknowledged and otherwise, which is not only a bad thing in itself but has had a pernicious influence on others, as can be seen from this essay.

He's a terrible man, no doubt of it, but also the best poet we've got — which may be awkward for critics, but perhaps we get the poets we deserve in Scotland as elsewhere. This is not the place to attempt an analysis of his poetry, which in my opinion is of the very highest quality in some instances and awesomely bad in others — he at least keeps to scale. Still, it may just be observed here that there is no lack of controversy about his poetry as about the rest of his activities. One might think otherwise from the line of patter passing for criticism in Scotland which devotes itself to the question of whether he is 'the greatest', or just one of the trinity with Burns and Dunbar, but the fact is that the various strata of his poems are very differently evaluated by different critics. There is a lively on-going debate about matters of quality and the relative importance of specific aspects of his development, even among his most convinced admirers, and a lot more criticism worthy of the name will need to be done before he is delivered over to the generalisations of the literary historians.

Since his self-confessed "over-indulgence in needless personalities" has been so often directed at distinguished figures of the Establishment, one would hardly expect him to have received many accolades in these quarters. "Probably the Scot who stands least in danger of receiving an LL.D. from a Scottish University," said William Power of him in 1931, thinking no doubt of the poet's then recently published lines:

> Losh! They'd ha' put me a brass plate up
> In Langholm Academy,
> And asked me to tak' the chair
> At mony a London Scots spree.
> They'd a' gien me my portrait in oils
> By Henry Kerr, and the LL.D. . . .
>> If I'd only had hokum, hokum,
>> Juist a wee thing common hokum!

One would be hard put to it to find evidence in the interim of his having acquired the approved line in hokum, but he did in fact get the LL.D. from Edinburgh University in 1957—a gesture which showed there was life yet in that venerable institution, whose Staff Club, moreover, houses a presentation portrait in oils which does no more justice to MacDiarmid, in my opinion (and, I am glad to say, that of his wife), than Henry Kerr's might have been expected to.

There is as yet no sign of a brass plate in his old school, Langholm Academy, though some of the citizens there have recently shown their determination to preserve the local library where he acquired for himself much of his early education, taking full advantage of the fact that he happened to live in the same building. But I have to confess to a sneaking regard for the thrawnness (or amplefeyst, as MacDiarmid might call it) of those Langholmites who, on observing that the rest of the world had begun to make a fuss over him, turned down a proposal that he should be given the freedom of his birthplace. One of the reasons given for this is said to be the allegation that he had done nothing for the burgh, the town council evidently being unappreciative of all that splendid verse and prose in which he has celebrated his native place. "What that meant," said MacDiarmid, "was that I hadn't presented Langholm with a couple of park benches or something of that sort." He reacted in predictable fashion, and the sequel has been recorded thus:

> Mr James Finlayson, of Hawick, as guest speaker proposing "The Immortal Memory" at the Eskdale Burns Club's supper in Langholm (January 1966), expressed the hope that a reconciliation might be effected between the author and his birthplace and that Langholm might not delay too long in honouring him, as Hawick had done in the case of the distinguished artist, Anne Redpath. Mr Finlayson's remarks were greeted with cries of "Never! Never!" and "Away back to Hawick".

But there's hope yet of a generation in Langholm who will share with the rest of us a due regard for the many passages in MacDiarmid's work which the greatness of the writer has offered to the spirit of the place — and there can be few left nowadays who are able to dismiss him on the traditional Scottish grounds that they "kent his faither". But there is one honour at least which one may doubt will ever come his way: that envisaged by his French admirer, Michel Habart, who said that "Dylan Thomas evokes somewhere 'all the statues that Scotland will one day put up to Hugh MacDiarmid', but let the latter beware lest England, in an access of humour, has the effrontery to erect a memorial to him in her turn. For from what crime of annexation would they shrink, that 'intensely vulgar race of infantile mind'?"

About all I can find to say for MacDiarmid's anti-Englishism is that the pro-English centres of power have been manipulating his country for so long that some such violent retaliation was inevitable. He himself puts it in perspective by listing his hobby in *Who's Who* as "Anglophobia". It is certainly deplorable in so far as it panders to the Scots' predilection for blaming on the English the mess into which they have allowed their country to degenerate. But MacDiarmid could reply that he has been willing to insult ninety-nine per cent of his own countrymen as readily as he has the English.

He does not *mention* the unmentionable: he broadcasts it over the tannoy. Back in 1936, when his fortunes were at a very low ebb, he was presented with a public testimonial, signed by Sir James Barrie, R. B. Cunninghame Graham, Compton Mackenzie, Lady Londonderry, Sir Herbert J. C. Grierson, Edward Garnett, Sean O'Casey and several hundred others, including, he has said, "practically every contemporary Scottish writer of any consequence whatever". The testimonial ran as follows:

> We, your fellow writers in Scotland and elsewhere, and other friends, whose signatures are appended hereto, desire to express our profound sense of the great services you have rendered to Scots letters and to literature in general.

> The place you have won as a poet is that of creative pioneer, inimitably bodying forth the form of things unknown, fusing passion and intellect, enlarging human and Scottish consciousness, and bringing your own country into vital touch with the main currents of world thought. Our appreciation of your genius is deepened by the fact that in your spontaneous self-expression you have expressed also the struggle of the Scots soul to regain a fuller and freer sense of the eternal universe of things. You are more than a "typical" Scot; you are the "different " Scot who, by the magic of a genius which is at the same time intimately Scottish and widely European, can raise native elements to a higher, a universal synthesis. It was through this power, exercised with passionate and gallant disinterestedness, and always with Scotland as the background and inspiration of your achievements, that you became a major force in the cultural and national life of your own country, supplying the dynamic of many forward movements.

> Genius is beyond calculation and above appraisement, but at least we can express our thankfulness that your high powers have been so closely allied with the intellectual cause of Scotland; and we can express also our admiration and esteem for a distinguished writer who has never swerved from his central purpose or failed to give kindly encouragement to anyone who had the highest interests of Scotland or its literature sincerely at heart.

> We trust that you may be spared for many years to bring fresh honour and inspiration to Scotland.

The recipient of this public tribute observed, a little later, that it was not wise to look a gift horse in the mouth. He then proceeded to do so. He was not in agreement, he said, with the wording of the testimonial, though not through any undue modesty. And he continued: "I had been personally friendly with many, perhaps most, of the writers who signed the testimonial, but I had now ceased to have any contacts whatever with most of them, and certainly could not have reciprocated their flattery to even the smallest extent. On the contrary, I was disappointed in those few of them of whom I had ever had any hope; most of the others I regarded as mere confounders of counsel and cumberers of the ground, intellectually, artistically and politically negligible where indeed they were not a positive nuisance. I had long known, if I had ever for a moment imagined otherwise, that I had nothing whatever in common with them. I realised too that the testimonial was likely to do me more harm than good. I have always had far more enemies than friends in Scotland — I should be greatly perturbed were it otherwise — and the former were always far more active than the latter — if indeed for the most part the latter were not so indistinguishable from the former as always to give me ample cause to cry, 'Deliver me from my friends'."

I await with interest his verdict on my temerity in having occasionally let slip a friendly word about him here. There are some who claim that he has mellowed in his eighties, but I would not rely on that. If true, it is probably only a passing phase.

One of the most extraordinary things about him is the fact that, despite his strenuous efforts to discourage it, he is held in deep and lasting affection by so many people, including not a few who say they have scars to show for it. There are vigilantes scattered far and near, earnestly endeavouring to dissuade him from doing *himself* further violent injury; and although he rarely allows his kindness any of the publicity so generously afforded his ferocity, I would venture to say that no one can be said properly to know him who has not experienced it.

To sum up, for myself the Scotland of my time without him is simply unimaginable. He has given me more delight, and more exasperation, than any other Scottish writer. I remember the editor of a student magazine giving as the prime reason why he liked living in Scotland the fact that Hugh MacDiarmid lives here: "It is surely good fortune to be a contemporary of one of the greatest Scotsmen ever, and in a time of national reawakening created largely by his efforts." May it long continue so, in both respects.

KENNETH BUTHLAY

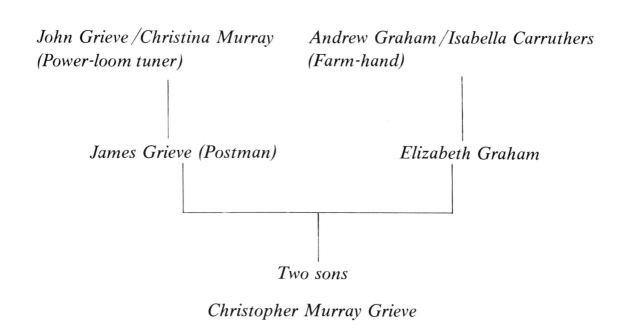

John Grieve /Christina Murray
(Power-loom tuner)

Andrew Graham /Isabella Carruthers
(Farm-hand)

James Grieve (Postman)

Elizabeth Graham

Two sons

Christopher Murray Grieve

Andrew Graham Grieve

Langholm in the 1890s.

C.M.G.'s maternal grandfather, Andrew Graham, his dog Turk, and Aunt Maggie, C.M.G.'s mother's youngest sister, at the door of Kirtleton Lodge, their home on Kirtleton Farm near Waterbeck, eighteen miles from Langholm. Andrew Graham worked as a farm-hand for most of his life and C.M.G. remembers his father hiring a pony and trap to take the family to visit his grandfather, a quiet, non-commital man, who had a family of eight. He died at the age of ninety-six after falling down the steps at the back of the lodge and breaking his neck. Aunt Maggie looked after the cheesery on the farm and died in 1948 at the age of ninety-four.

*Photo: J. Warwick*

C.M.G. was delivered by Dr John Gill at the family home in Arkinholm Terrace, Langholm, on 11th August 1892. This first photograph with his parents was taken in Carlisle in the autumn of 1892. His mother described him as "an eaten an' spewed lookin' wee thing wi' een like twa burned holes in a blanket".

The Town Hall,
Langholm, 1895.

*Photo: Courtesy Matt Ewart*

The Post office and
Library Buildings,
Langholm, 1895.

*Photo: Courtesy Matt Ewart*

High Street,
Langholm, 1890.

*Photo: Courtesy Ewart Library,
Dumfries*

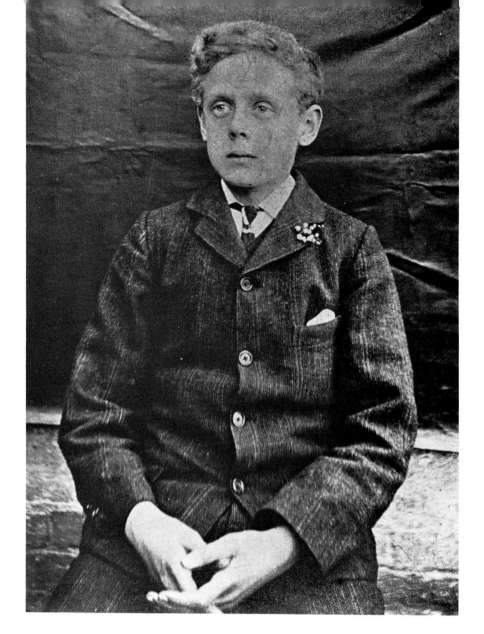

C.M.G. aged about eleven. Photograph by amateur photographer Eddie Armstrong, a postman colleague of C.M.G.'s father.

In 1896, the family moved to a house in Henry Street and at the age of five C.M.G. was enrolled at Langholm infant school. At the age of seven he entered the primary department of Langholm Academy where he was taught general subjects by Francis George Scott. F. G. Scott was also the music master for the school and promoted musical events in the academy.

In the same year the family moved to another house in Library Buildings, Parliament Square, which was situated at street level behind the post office where his father was employed as a postman and below the town library where his mother was employed as caretaker.

C.M.G. had permanent access to the library and as he grew, he developed a tremendous appetite for reading material. He had the ability to read at speed and would take a clothes basket upstairs to the library to select a week's supply of books. The librarian at this time was Maggie Cairns who was married to C.M.G.'s cousin, John Laidlaw.

At the age of twelve C.M.G. (known to all the locals as Kirsty) was transferred to the secondary department of the Academy where he played rugby and hockey and enjoyed fishing in his spare time, but his main interests were his literary pursuits and he continued to read extensively and develop his writing.

Langholm South U.F. Church Sunday School picnic to Burnfoot, Eskdalemuir, in 1905. An open coach trip with sports, buns and tea. C.M.G. extreme left, back row, with hat, buttonhole and cigarette.

C.M.G.'s father was a church elder and superintendent of the Sunday school and C.M.G. was brought up in the ways of the kirk. At the age of thirteen, C.M.G. was teaching the tiny tots in Sunday school and was awarded many certificates for Bible knowledge. One evening each week, he attended Bible class at the home of the Rev. Thomas Scott Cairncross, a man with a keen literary interest who reviewed books for the *Irish Times* and indeed wrote poetry and was published himself. The Rev. Cairncross had a fine library and allowed C.M.G. to borrow from his collection. New books were financially out of reach for C.M.G., and the income of review copies to the Rev. Cairncross proved to be a literary gold mine.

C.M.G.'s first published poem appeared in the local *Eskdale and Liddesdale Advertiser* about this time. He also contributed articles on the genealogy of local families and researched the work of William Julius Meikle who supposedly wrote the song "There's nae luck aboot the hoose".

However, C.M.G. was starting to question his religious training.

*Photo: Eddie Armstrong*                              George Ogilvie

On 2nd September 1908 at the age of sixteen, C.M.G. was admitted as a pupil teacher to Broughton Higher Grade School and Junior Student Centre, Macdonald Road, Edinburgh. George Ogilvie, an Ayrshire man, was principal teacher of English at Broughton (nicknamed "Cholly" by the students) and taught a wide range of Scottish literature and the English romantic poets. He soon began to realise the potential of his new pupil and started to take a particular interest in C.M.G. Ogilvie was a socialist and C.M.G. was often invited to his home in Cluny Gardens for evening discussions on literature and politics. In the same year C.M.G. joined the Edinburgh Central Branch of the Independent Labour Party of Great Britain and the Edinburgh University branch of the socialist and literary debating Fabian Society.

C.M.G. edited *The Broughton Magazine,* Vol. 3 Nos. 1-3, Christmas 1909 to summer 1910. There were few contributors to the magazine (although C.M.G. would spend time canvassing in the corridors after the English class), so he had to write sufficient material himself to fill the magazine. It was also part of the editor's job to solicit advertising, if possible, enough to cover the printing costs.

In a tribute to C.M.G. in the Christmas 1920 issue of *The Broughton Magazine* George Ogilvie wrote:

"I remember vividly Grieve's arrival amongst us. I see the little, slimly built figure in hodden grey, the small, sharp-featured face with its piercing eyes, the striking head with its broad brow and great mass of flaxen curly hair. He hailed from Langholm, and had a Border accent you could have cut with a knife. I am afraid some of the city students smiled at first at the newcomer, but he very speedily won their respect. He certainly very quickly established himself in mine. His first essay (an unseen done in class) is still to my mind the finest bit of work I have got in Broughton. The subject was "A Country Road",

25

and Grieve hedged it with the wayside beauty and paved it with the golden romance of the Borders. You may be sure that I made it my chief business from that day onwards to keep my eye on Grieve. He did not belie the promise of his start. The wider circle of Broughton rapidly drew out and developed his gifts; very soon, by common consent, he took his place as leader of the Centre. He was the life and soul of the Literary Society and ready at a moment's notice to write a poem or make a speech. His sparkling trail, naturally, runs through the magazine of those years. He wrote poetry and prose with equal facility; indeed, his facility was positively uncanny, and the amazing thing was that everything he did was superlatively good. That is, everything he did in the line of literature. He was not, it must be admitted, a model student; in some subjects, frankly, he had no interest. As a matter of fact he became the despair of most of his teachers. Yet none of them could help liking him. He had a most engaging ingenuousness, and I have yet to meet the infant who could look as innocent as Grieve.

Grieve was a predestined editor of our magazine, and here is how he inaugurated his editorship in his first preface:"

HOW often have we given to the breezes the biscuit-coloured bag that erstwhile held our " piece "—watched it flutter like an abnormal young canary—almost graze the red flagstones—then, with great shouting of the winds, climb the noon-tinted air and float away over and behind the blue-grey roof of yonder skyscraper—with what rapture on our lips, tho' one cold-tongued scientist might swear 'twould somewhere kiss the dust again, by Newton's eternal pippin !

Two Editors have given sets of Broughtonian bags to the winds of popularity, and safely have they been borne above the green slates of Broughton and twined, to the confusion of certain cloak-room "Newtonians," about the weather-cock for aye—the yellow ensigns of of our culture.  A new Editor lets the first bag of the third set timidly from his fingers, grateful to the Headmaster for the lusty " speeding " he gives it.  The H.G. bellows, and the fans of the Centre and F.P.'s, are doing their duty (tho' a bigger bellows and a few more fans might easily be bought), and the Editor watches the weather-cock from a corridor window.  *Floreat Brotoniensis!*

Only the lungs of enthusiastic co-operation can blow our Magazine above the weather-cock of precarious life, up among the white clouds of success ; and only a strong magazine-spirit, permeating each unit of the " concentric circles " of F.P.'s, the Centre and the Higher Grade, and raising our circulation from the meagre actual to the goodly possible, will keep it there, resisting that gravity-like force which is ever tending to pull our yellow venture down again to that grey level whence it started.

"The cleverest thing that Grieve did during his editorship was a couple of poems for his last number of the magazine, which also marked the close of his attendance at Broughton. He announced to me (as many other editors of the "B.M." have done on the eve of going to press) that he had not enough MSS., and asked me (as many other editors of the "B.M." have done) to come to his rescue. Whereupon I sat down and wrote "two valedictory poems by any teacher to any pupil leaving Broughton", one in serious and the other in humorous vein. I handed them to Grieve. He read them, sat down, and in an incredibly short space of time ran off "Two valedictory poems to any teacher from any pupil leaving Broughton" like mine, one grave, one gay. Here they are:

# Two Valedictory Poems

## From any Teacher to any Pupil leaving School

### I. GRAVE.

The cape is rounded and the white waves run
About the eager keel. The slack sails ope,
And like a 'scapèd bird a-flutter with hope,
The good ship trembles in its joy new-won.
The long, slow miles adown the firth are done,
No more the shallows and the tethering rope
And furl'd sails; but all the wide sea's scope
To voyage on beneath the stars and sun.

The pilot's boat drops fast astern. He stands
And feels through all his blood the spell o' the sea
And happy havens of the far-set isles.

Then with the smile of God when from His hands
He launches white souls on the vast to-be,
He patiently rethreads the long, slow miles.

### II. GAY.

"Farewell, we have been long together,
In sunshine and in cloudy weather"—
And incidentally we've learned a good deal each of either.

I cannot say you are a scholar
On whom I'd bet my bottom dollar:
Your neck has never fitted quite the pedagogic collar.

But you have been a rare good fellow,
Whate'er your sex, female or male O!
And I've the greatest pleasure now in wishing you farewell O!

# Two Valedictory Poems

## To any Teacher from any Pupil leaving School

### I. GRAVE.

Pilot, farewell! By labyrinthine ways
Down to the deep'ning of uncharted seas
Thou hast me led. On flashing seas like these
Did dreaming young Columbus big-eyed gaze.
Shall I sail on up level-shining rays
Into yon red sun which is Death-in-peace,
My sails filled with that buoyant breeze
Which blows from out the freshness of one's days?

The winds of youth may fail, my sails fall slack,
These paths to Splendid Death like arrows fly
Into a night wherein the sun goes black.

My prow is set unchangeably. Good-bye!
My soul's star keeps me to a turnless track.
My haven's at the far end of the sky.

### II. GAY.

Sir, you're very like a comet
Whose orbit is a closed ellipse.
The phlegm with which you roam it
Gives me pips.

If you had any soul you know,
At either of your foci,
You'd burst th' ellipse and go
In a hyperbola—to hockey.

We've had a lot of mutual patience,
You and I, through all these years.
And after all on these occasions
It's fairly easy to dispense with tears.

"You may take my word for it that Grieve carried off the honours in the exchange of compliments. But the important point to note is the vein of poetry revealed in the first of the two poems. This is the vein that he has been working in his subsequent poetry, and in a sequence of fifty sonnets he sent me the other day I find poetic ore of rich and rare quality. His work has acquired beauty and power beyond even my fondest expectations."

In 1910 at the age of eighteen, C.M.G. left Broughton and for several weeks worked as a freelance journalist from his parents' home in Langholm. Through the recommendations of George Ogilvie he was offered employment as a journalist with the *Edinburgh Evening Dispatch* and worked there for a year before returning to Langholm to freelance again.

On 3rd February 1911, C.M.G.'s father, James Grieve, died of pneumonia at the age of forty-seven.

In October 1911, C.M.G. left Scotland for South Wales to take up a position with the *Monmouthshire Labour News* where he worked for several months living in lodgings in Ebbw Vale.

C.M.G. then returned to Langholm and lived with his widowed mother. His writing brought in around £1 per week, which allowed him to smoke and purchase newspapers.

In a letter to George Ogilvie in 1916, C.M.G. recalled this period. "Philandered extensively. . . . Intimate passages with three young ladies, all English, revived in me our racial antipathy to the English, which, recurring lately, has caused me to write quite a body (some thirty poems in all) of anti-English verse, not dissimilar to certain products of Irish revival. More important is the way in which my attention for the first time turned to Scottish Nationalism and national problems. . . ."

C.M.G. then found work with the *Clydebank and Renfrew Press* and moved to live in Clydebank. He described the post as "a cushie job, but poorly paid", although he lived a strenuous life there for around five months with little time for reading or original writing. He did however rejoin the Independent Labour Party, having let his membership lapse and became friends with James Maxton and other prominent members of the socialist movement.

Meantime, his brother had secured an option for him on a job in Cupar at a much higher wage and he moved into the post of an assistant editor of the three associated newspapers, *The Fife Herald, St Andrews Citizen* and *Fife Coast Chronicle*. It was in this office that he first met Peggy Skinner, a copyholder, who was to become his wife in 1918.

However, C.M.G. did not get on well with one of the bosses and "a rupture beyond repair" sent him to Forfar.

Renting a house four miles into the country by Glamis Castle, his mother moved in to keep house for him. The result was extremely satisfactory, he now had an easy well-paid job with the *Forfar Review* and peace to write and court Peggy Skinner.

At the outbreak of war in 1914 many young men had volunteered for service and by 1915 it was becoming increasingly more difficult for a young man physically fit to remain in civvies.

*Photo: Laing*

In July 1915, C.M.G. reported to Hillsborough Barracks, Sheffield, and joined the army. Within six months he had risen from a recruit to be acting quarter-master sergeant of a company one thousand strong.

In 1916 he was sent to Aldershot with the last acting rank of Q.M.S. and came through in orders with the substantive (permanent) rank of sergeant and was detailed to proceed with his unit which he did early in August 1916.

C.M.G. is pictured above with his mother in Forfar before going abroad to Salonica where he served as sergeant 64020 in the 42nd General Hospital, R.A.M.C., as a night ward master.

Throughout his service abroad he continued to correspond with George Ogilvie, sending him poetry for his critical evaluation and exchanging general information.

Mrs Peggy Grieve,
photographed in
W.R.A.A.C. uniform
shortly after her
marriage to C.M.G. in 1918.

In September 1916, C.M.G. suffered his first attack of malaria. He was treated and able to continue with his duties for about eighteen months but eventually his condition deteriorated and in April 1918, he was invalided home to the Malaria Concentration Centre, near Rhyl, North Wales.

After two months at Rhyl, C.M.G. was rehabilitated and classed fit. Taking the opportunity of a few days' leave he and Peggy decided to marry and on the 13th June 1918, the Rev. R. J. Drummond, of Lothian Road Church, Edinburgh, performed the ceremony at his manse in Edinburgh. Peggy was at this time serving in the W.R.A.A.C. as secretary to the Colonel of the Black Watch at Queen's Barracks, Perth.

C.M.G. was then posted to Sections Lahore Indian General Hospital at Estaque near Marseilles in France. This was a native labour hospital which dealt in the repatriation of Asiatics.

There were around three hundred mentally disturbed Asiatics in his care with a high mortality rate. C.M.G. was responsible for indenting logs and mutton fat each morning and supervising the cremation of the night's dead. The hospitals were serviced with Gurkhas who carried out the work. Medical supplies included brandy and rum which C.M.G. indented for administration to sick Sikhs. Unfortunately, the Sikhs were religiously teetotal and refused their medication. However, in these lean years of the war nothing was allowed to waste.

On demob in July 1919, C.M.G. joined his wife in St Andrews where she was employed as a secretary with a firm of solicitors. They lived in lodgings in St Andrews for a short while until C.M.G. found work as a reporter with *The Montrose Review* and moved to lodgings in Montrose where Peggy joined him a few weeks later.

After a period working for *The Montrose Review,* C.M.G. was offered employment with Ross and Cromarty Education Authority as headmaster of a side school at Kildermorie, a deer forest and lodge ten miles north-west of Alness in E. Ross and Cromarty, to teach the two daughters of the head stalker there.

C.M.G. accepted the offer and he and his wife moved north in October 1920 and were accommodated in one of the shooting lodges a short distance from the school.

In a letter to George Ogilvie, C.M.G. wrote, "Although I was flourishing financially and socially (in Montrose) I was not getting sufficient leisure for original work and consequently verging upon a breakdown." Kildermorie was twelve miles from the nearest village, Boath, and the solitude allowed him to concentrate more fully on his writing. In another letter to Ogilvie (15th November 1920) he wrote, "Poetic output has run away with me lately, including sonnets, over one hundred and twenty in less than five weeks." During his stay at Kildermorie C.M.G. undertook secretarial work for Mr Dyson Perrins of Ardross Castle, the Worcester Sauce millionaire. Mr Dyson Perrins had a collection of fine books and C.M.G. was employed to catalogue them.

In April 1921 *The Montrose Review* offered C.M.G. his old job at an increased salary and he and his wife returned to Montrose to live in lodgings at 19 Kincardine Street and 12 White's Place before settling into a new council house at 16 Links Avenue on 17th March 1922, where they remained for the rest of their stay in Montrose.

At the beginning of 1922, C.M.G. was elected to the town council of Montrose as an Independent Socialist and became a hospital master, an old office which put him in charge of the mortifications and charities administered by the council. He also became a parish councillor, a member of the School Management Committee and in 1926 was appointed Justice of the Peace in which capacity he performed non-religious ceremonies.

Fortunately, all this work for Montrose could easily be combined with his work as a reporter as he was always at the centre of happenings of local interest. Life was busy but enjoyable and he managed to fit innumerable interests into a working day.

At the beginning of 1922, C.M.G. was waiting for T. N. Foulis to publish his first book, *Annals of the Five Senses*, but the publishers encountered financial difficulties and the manuscript was eventually returned. C.M.G. decided to undertake the expense of publication to avoid further delay and the first edition was published from his address at 16 Links Avenue in June 1923.

Mrs Peggy Grieve found Montrose rather dull and expressed a desire to live in Edinburgh. C.M.G. explored the possibilities of working there and when the post of Keeper of the National Gallery of Scotland was advertised in *The Glasgow Herald* early in 1925 he applied with the support of several people and the sponsorship of John Buchan. His application was unsuccessful.

C.M.G. was content in Montrose and enjoyed good health. In a letter to George Ogilvie (9th December 1926) he wrote, "As a matter of fact I keep wonderfully fit. I have not had a doctor since I left the army in 1919 and no illness of any real consequence. I am frankly anxious not to die young. In many ways I am a late ripener. All my best work is still to come, I am only beginning to find myself."

*Photo: D. C. Thomson*

The town of Montrose in the late 1920s.

---

# MONTROSE: By HUGH MacDIARMID

**The following poem on "Montrose" by C. M. Grieve (Hugh MacDiarmid) was specially commissioned by the "Review" for publication in the 150th Anniversary number. C. M. Grieve is undoubtedly Scotland's most celebrated and controversial poet.**

*Where better could a town be placed than here?*
*Peninsular Montrose has everything*
*With water on three sides, while, beyond*
*Rich farmlands, the hills upswing.*

*It has the right size too—not a huge*
*Sprawling mass, but compact as a heart,*
*Life-supplier to a whole diversified area*
*Yet with the economy of a work of art.*

*So small that it is possible to know*
*Everyone in it, yet it still radiates*
*In ties not broken but strengthened*
*To successive generations of expatriates.*

*So small and yet radiating out*
*Not only in space but in time, since here*
*History gives permanence of distinction*
*And dignity to each succeeding year.*

*"Guid gear gangs in sma' book" and fegs!*
*Man's story owes more to little towns than to great.*
*And Montrose is typical of Scotland's small grey*
*   burghs*
*Each with a character of its own time cannot*
*   abate.*

*Model of the preference of quality to quantity*
*Montrose set here between the hills and the sea*
*On its tongue of land is a perfect example*
*Of multum in parvo—Earth's best in epitome.*

---

The above poem was specially commissioned by *The Montrose Review* for publication in the 150th anniversary number, 12th January 1961.

Corresponding with C.M.G. during his service abroad, George Ogilvie had suggested the possibility of publishing an annual anthology of contemporary Scottish poets. When C.M.G. returned to Scotland he approached T. N. Foulis, the Edinburgh publishers, who were immediately impressed with the idea and commissioned C.M.G. to collect and edit the contents of a first edition.

C.M.G. advertised for contributions and Helen B. Cruickshank replied, submitting some of her verse and they began to correspond.

*Northern Numbers* First Series was published in 1920 in both hardback and paperback format as was Series Two, published in 1921, but before Series Three could be published T. N. Foulis were declared bankrupt. To save the situation C.M.G. took over Series Three and published it in 1922 in a limited edition of four hundred copies paperback at his own expense from his address in Montrose.

The publication of the three volumes of *Northern Numbers* heralded the start of the Scottish Literary Renaissance. Here gathered for the first time were Scottish writers striving to establish better standards in poetic performance, and the public were beginning to take notice.

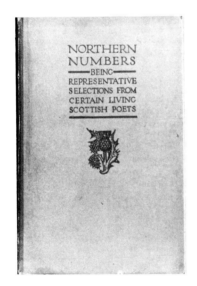
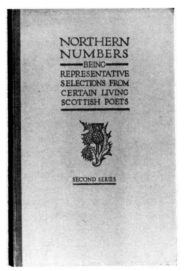

In 1923, PEN International was founded in London by Mrs Dawson Scott, the poet and novelist, PEN stands for poets, playwrights, editors, essayists, novelists. C.M.G. joined shortly after, and during meetings in London he met Rebecca West, John Galsworthy, George Bernard Shaw, H. G. Wells and Cunninghame Graham.

In 1924 C.M.G. met Helen B. Cruickshank for the first time at "Ravelston Elms", the Edinburgh home of Pittendrigh Macgillivray, the sculptor-poet.

On the 6th September 1924 Peggy gave birth to their first child, Christine.

In 1925 Wm. Blackwood and Sons, of Edinburgh, published *Sangschaw*, the first collection of poems by Hugh MacDiarmid. In 1926 they published two other collections, *Penny Wheep* and *A Drunk Man Looks at the Thistle*.

C

  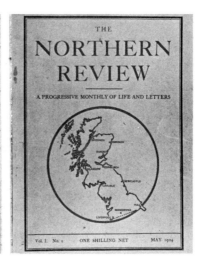

On 26th August 1922, C.M.G. edited and published from 16 Links Avenue, Montrose, the first issue of a new monthly Scottish literary magazine, *The Scottish Chapbook*, described on the magazine's letterhead as "a high-class monthly devoted to Scottish Arts and Letters". The magazine's slogan was "Not Traditions — Precedents!". The first number, which sold out immediately, contained a poem, "A Moment in Eternity" by C. M. Grieve, dedicated to George Ogilvie, and the first part of a play script, "Nisbet, An Interlude in Post-War Glasgow" by Hugh MacDiarmid, which was concluded in the second issue. In the third issue of the magazine, October 1922, the poem "The Watergaw" by Hugh MacDiarmid, appeared. This was the first time C.M.G. had published one of his poems using the pseudonym Hugh MacDiarmid.

*The Scottish Chapbook* ceased publication with the issue for November/December 1923.

On 8th May 1923 C.M.G. edited and published the first issue of *The Scottish Nation* to propagate Scottish Nationalism. The magazine was issued for thirty-four weeks and ceased publication with the issue for 25th December 1923.

*The Northern Review*, a Progressive Monthly of Life and Letters", was edited by C.M.G. and published in Edinburgh. The first issue appeared in May 1924 but only ran to four monthly issues.

After leaving Langholm Academy in 1908, C.M.G. lost touch with Francis George Scott, his primary master, and it was not until his first MacDiarmid lyrics appeared in *The Scottish Chapbook* that they were to meet again.

It so happened that an English teacher who was at Langholm Academy with Scott and taught C.M.G., Mr William Burt, subsequently of Linlithgow Academy, saw several MacDiarmid poems (which he thought to be the pen of C.M.G.) in *The Scottish Chapbook* and sent copies to Scott. He also wrote to C.M.G., who came to Linlithgow to visit, and F. G. Scott joined them the next day.

It was a great reunion, Mr Burt's three-year-old son Billy recited one of C.M.G.'s poems, and later, C.M.G. wrote the poem "Hungry Waters" for him. F.G., not to be outdone, set it to music.

Scott at once realised he had found what he was looking for, a Scottish lyrical poet whose lyrics were exactly the type he wanted to set. He and C.M.G. became very close friends and Scott eventually made song settings of about seventy MacDiarmid poems.

William Burt and Francis George Scott photographed in St Andrews.

## HUNGRY WATERS

FOR A LITTLE BOY AT LINLITHGOW

The auld men o' the sea
Wi' their daberlack hair
Ha'e dackered the coasts
O' the country fell sair.

They gobble owre cas'les,
Chow mountains to san';
Or lang they'll eat up
The haill o' the lan'.

Lickin' their white lips
An' yowlin' for mair,
The auld men o' the sea
Wi' their daberlack hair.

*Photo: Kenneth M. Hay*

The bronze bust of C.M.G. by William Lamb, A.R.S.A., sculpted in Montrose in 1925. Only one cast has been made and this is on view at the William Lamb Museum, Montrose.

Edwin Muir, Francis George Scott and his eldest son, George, and C.M.G., photographed in Montrose in 1924. Edwin and his wife, Willa, had just returned from Prague where Edwin was employed with The British Council and they were living in the High Street where Willa's mother had a shop. F. G. Scott and his family were visiting on holiday. C.M.G. was working on his long poem sequence, *A Drunk Man Looks at the Thistle*, at this time, and F.G. was following his progress with great interest. He had already set several of C.M.G.'s lyrics to music with great effect.

TO

## F. G. SCOTT

Can ratt-rime and ragments o' quenry
And recoll o' Gillha' requite
Your faburdoun, figuration, and gemmell,
And prick-sangs' delight?

Tho' you've cappilowed me in the reapin'
— And yours was a bursten kirn tae! —
Yet you share your advantage wi' me
In the end o' the day.

And my flytin' and sclatrie sall be
Wi' your fantice and mocage entwined
As the bauch Earth is wi' the lift
Or fate wi' mankind!

**Councillor CHRISTOPHER M. GRIEVE**

*Photo: A. S. Milne*

# A Christmas Carol.

## O JESU PARVULE

*" Followis ane sang of the birth of Christ, with the tune of Baw lu la law."*
—" Godly Ballates."

His mither sings to the bairnie Christ
Wi' the tune o' *Baw lu la law.*
The bonnie wee craturie lauchs in His crib
An' a' the starnies and He are sib.
            *Baw, baw, my loonikie, baw, balloo.*

"Fa' owre, ma hinny, fa' owre, fa' owre,
A' body's sleepin' binna oorsels."
She's drawn Him in tae the bool o' her breist
But the byspale's nae thocht o' sleep i' the least.
            *Balloo, wee mannie, balloo, balloo.*

sib = blood relation.     binna = except.     bool = curve.     byspale = wonderful child.

BROUGHTON has reason to be proud of her son and former Editor, C. M. Grieve, who, writing under the pseudonym of Hugh M'Diarmid, has just published a volume entitled "Sangschaw" (Blackwood & Sons, 5s.) from which the above poem is reprinted with the author's permission. It is an excellent example of M'Diarmid's art. He is best in short lyrics like this and the volume is full of them. Each poem, from *Reid E'en* and *Moonlight Among the Pines*, with their romanticism, to *Country Life* and *Crowdieknowe*, with their humorous realism, and to *Cophetua*, with its satire, is in itself a little masterpiece.

M'Diarmid's work, although an experiment in a new type of Scots poetry, is a complete success at the first venture. He has shown us that Scots is still a suitable, and a highly successful, medium of expression for all kinds of verse. He does not confine himself to the dialect of any one district, but judiciously selects words and idioms used anywhere between the Cheviots and the Moray Firth  The result is Scots which no Scot, no matter how extensively he has read Scots poetry, can get through without consulting the glossary. But the beauty of these poems is more than ample compensation.

Unlike many recent dialect writers, M'Diarmid is no kail-yard poet. Not only do we find much sly, quiet humour in him, but also a seriousness and a vein of philosophy absent in most Scots poets. His appeal, and in this respect he has much in common with Burns, is universal. As proof of this we need only mention that most of the poems have already been translated into French and Danish, an honour which few living, especially young, British poets can claim. Indeed, Grieve's experiment has received such a welcome, that we need have no doubts concerning the success of the Scottish Renaissance Movement which he leads.          J. K. A.

"Sangshaw", reviewed by J. K. Annand, editor of *The Broughton Magazine*, in the December issue, 1925.

16 Links Avenue.
Montrose.
2nd June, 1926

My dear Annand.

Herewith translation, and your original. I am very sensible of our kindness to me in all this, and am looking eagerly forward to the issue. Be sure and keep aside a number of copies for me. There are several people to whom I shall want to send one.

No more just now! I'm just scrawling this off in haste, as I've been too long in letting you have this already. but I've been living in an awful rush these past few weeks.

I enclose a poem just written in case you do want one to the Magazine's very own cheek. But, if not, or if it's too late, or otherwise unsuitable, never mind.

Best wishes. Yours. C. M. Grieve

A letter from C.M.G. to J. K. Annand (then editing *The Broughton Magazine*) returning a translation of Annand's editorial for a Braid Scots issue of the magazine which Annand had written in English and C.M.G. translated into Scots, and submitting a poem for the magazine.

# Yet Hae I Silence Left.

Yet hae I Silence left, the croon o' a'.

Tho' her, wha on the hills langsyne I saw
liftin' a forehead o' perpetual snaw.

Tho' her, wha in the how-dumb-deid o' nicht
Kythes, like Eternity in Time's despite.

Tho' her, withooten shape, whas name is Daith.

Tho' Him, unkennable abies by faith.

— God whom, gin e'er He saw a man 'ud be
Ten mair dumfooner't at the sicht than he!

But Him, whom nocht in Man or Deity
Or Daith or Dreid or laneliness can touch,
Wha's deed owre often and has seen owre much.

O I hae Silence left, the croon o' a'.

Hugh M'Diarmid.

(italic)

The stanzas submitted are a draft of the conclusion of *A Drunk Man Looks at the Thistle*, which was published on the 22nd November of that year. Unfortunately, the poem arrived too late for inclusion in the magazine.

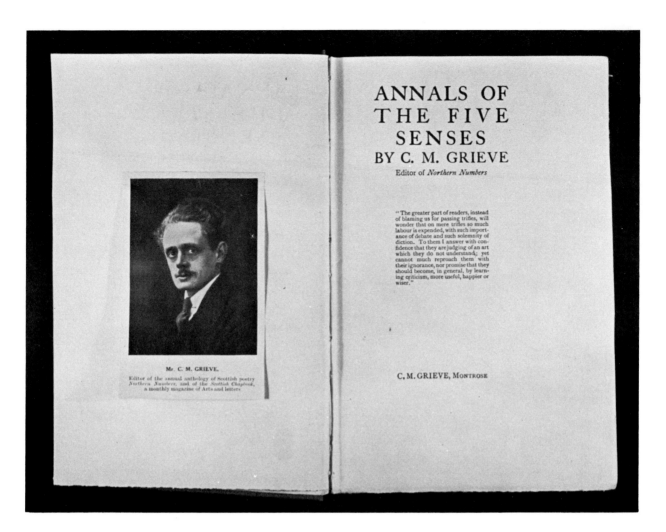

C.M.G.'s first book, *Annals of the Five Senses*, which he published himself in 1923. The illustration is a newspaper cutting of the period.

## THE WATERGAW

Ae weet forenicht i' the yow-trummle
I saw yon antrin thing,
A watergaw wi' its chitterin' licht
Ayont the on-ding;
An' I thocht o' the last wild look ye gied
Afore ye deed!

There was nae reek i' the laverock's hoose
That nicht — an' nane i' mine;
But I hae thocht o' that foolish licht
Ever sin' syne;
An' I think that mebbe at last I ken
What your look meant then.

Studio photograph by Andrew Paterson of Inverness, January 1927.

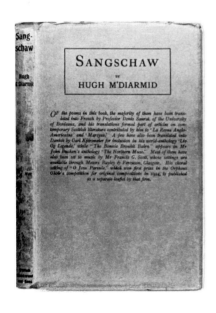

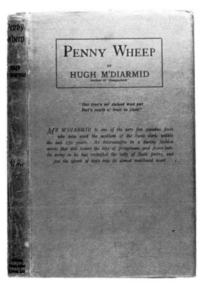

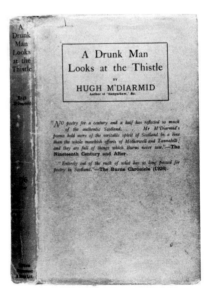

9th September 1925
5/-

16th June 1926
5/-

22nd November 1926
7/6

Studio photograph by Andrew Paterson of Inverness, January 1927.

In 1927, John Galsworthy, who was the first president of the English Centre of PEN, asked his friend Herbert Grierson, then Professor of English Literature and Rhetoric at Edinburgh University, to consider founding a centre for Scotland. C.M.G. was approached with the idea and agreed to organise an inaugural meeting. C.M.G. invited all his literary contacts in Scotland to attend a meeting in the Grosvenor Hotel in Glasgow in the summer of that year, and by the end of the meeting, a committee had been formed and C.M.G. elected secretary. Lady Margaret Sackville, daughter of Earl de la Warr, accepted the invitation to become the first president of the Scottish Centre of PEN, which was administered from C.M.G.'s address in Montrose.

Early members of the Scottish Centre were R. B. Cunninghame Graham, Compton Mackenzie, William Power, William Soutar, William Jeffrey, Marion Angus, Marion Lochhead, Herbert Grierson and Helen B. Cruickshank.

C.M.G. organised monthly meetings of PEN either in Edinburgh or Glasgow and always stayed with Helen Cruickshank and her mother over the Saturday night when the meetings were in Edinburgh, sleeping in the tiny front room at "Dinnieduff" with its sloping roof, which Mrs Cruickshank christened "The Prophet's Chamber" after the story of Elijah and the pious widow who always placed her small "chamber in the wall" at the prophet's disposal. Mrs Cruickshank was pleased to see C.M.G. as he brought news of Montrose and her nephew, Major William Wood, who also served on the town council.

C.M.G., Sir Herbert Grierson and William Power represented the new Scottish Centre of PEN at an international congress in Oslo. Delegates from other countries could not understand why the Scots were not content to stay within the London Centre, and on their return to Scotland, William Power proposed the constitution of a Gaelic-speaking section, which was formed but was hardly ever operative. It did however emphasise that Scotland had a separate language and culture from England, and was worthy of individual representation at an international conference.

### PEN (Scottish Centre) 21st April 1928

President—Lady Margaret Sackville
Secretary—C. M. Grieve
Treasurer—Alexander McGill

Committee
(Edinburgh Section)
Dr Pittendrigh Macgillivray
Prof. Herbert Grierson
Lewis Spence
Helen B. Cruickshank

(Glasgow Section)
William Power
Marion Lochhead
Edward Scouller
J. M. Reid

# NATIONAL
# Demonstration

IN SUPPORT OF A

## Scottish Parliament

# KING'S PARK, Stirling
# SATURDAY, 23rd JUNE, 3 p.m.

SPEAKERS:

# R. B. Cunninghame Graham, J.P., D.L.
# Hon. R. Erskine of Marr
# Compton Mackenzie, O.B.E.
# Lewis Spence   C. M. Grieve, J.P.

AND OTHERS

# McLEAN PIPE BAND
### (WORLD'S CHAMPIONS, COWAL, 1927).

ALL WELCOME :: :: COLLECTION

Y.M.C.A. HALL, Dumbarton Road, has
been reserved in the event of wet weather.

George Spens, Printer, 31 Glassford Street, Glasgow, C.1.                [P.T.O.]

# INAUGURATION DEMONSTRATION

OF THE

# NATIONAL PARTY OF SCOTLAND

Held in King's Park, Stirling, on Saturday, 23rd June, 1928

---

Carried forward on a spate of oratory and to the accompaniment of strains from the World's Champion Pipers, the Clan M'Lean Pipe Band, the new National Party of Scotland was inaugurated at a demonstration held in the King's Park, Stirling, on Saturday, 23rd June, 1928. The gathering coincided with the anniversary of the battle of Bannockburn. Mr. R. B. Cunninghame Graham, J.P., D.L., the National Party's candidate in the coming Rectorial contest at Glasgow University, presided over the gathering, and was supported amongst others by H. Balderstone (Glasgow); Donald Clark (Inverkeithing); Hon. R. Erskine of Marr (Aboyne); T. H. Gibson (Strathaven); C. M. Grieve, J.P. (Montrose); Miss H. H. Guthrie (Leith); W. K. Lyon, W.S. (Edinburgh); D. C. MacKechnie (Glasgow); John M. MacCormick, M.A. (Glasgow); Miss A. Milne (Glasgow); Mr. and Mrs. Moffat (Bridge of Weir); W. G. Burn Murdoch (Edinburgh); Mr. and Mrs. Hugh Paterson (Coupar Angus); Miss Simpson (Dundee); W. Stewart Carmichael (Dundee); Mr. and Mrs. Lewis Spence (Edinburgh); James Valentine (Glasgow).

Mr. Lewis Spence said:—Mr. Chairman, Scotsmen and Scotswomen, it is my pleasant duty to move the following resolution:—

"That this meeting, having regard to present conditions in Scotland and the imperative need for the reconstruction of Scottish National life, expresses its strong conviction that this can only be achieved by the obtaining of such powers of Self-government as will ensure to Scotland independent National status within the British group of Nations, approves of the formation of the National Party of Scotland, whose policy is directed to this end, and hereby pledges itself to support actively all candidates put forward by that Party in both Parliamentary and Local Government Elections."
(Applause.)

Mr C. M. Grieve said:—Mr. Chairman, Ladies and Gentlemen, I must follow the example of my forerunners in speaking to-day by removing my hat, although my hair is perhaps less amenable than even the Chairman's. (Laughter.)
I rise to second the Resolution that Mr. Spence has moved in the absence of my friend, Mr. Compton Mackenzie. I know that Mr. Mackenzie will be exceedingly sorry to miss this gathering to-day, and that the interest which he is taking in the Scottish National Movement is a very genuine and a very deep one. While I am, of course, in entire sympathy with the Resolution, I do not feel that I am particularly called upon to say anything more to commend it to you than has already been said for it. I feel that although they have their uses, Resolutions in themselves do not matter a great deal. I have a recollection of a very long process of Resolution passing, and what I came to seek for to-day was the Resolution behind the

Resolution — the Resolution of the people who are going to support the Resolution. When you compare this gathering, excellent though it is, with the twenty or thirty thousand who gathered the other week at Dundas Castle to hear a Worcestershire farmer tell you all that he misapprehended about Scotland, or compare it with the amateur theatricals that are going on to-day at Garscube, where Scotsmen — save the mark — are imitating traditions in relation to which they are negligible, it may seem that this Scottish National Movement is not making any great headway.

But it is making very real headway, and this meeting is no adequate reflection of the progress that is being made or of the changed nature of Scottish Nationalism to-day.

Undoubtedly the question of Scottish Nationalism and the position of the Scottish National Party is going to be a very live issue at the next General Election. Funds are coming in, and men are coming in. There is a most remarkable return to Scotland of men whom force of circumstances, whom the Anglicisation of our country has wrested away from interest in Scottish affairs they are sub-consciously touched to-day, and they are returning to a new interest in Scotland. Mr. MacCormick has alluded to the young people in Scotland.

Perhaps one of the best signs of the new trend in Scottish affairs is the formation of that Association which Mr. MacCormick so ably represents, the Glasgow University Nationalist Association. It is a great change in Scottish affairs to find a Nationalist Association in connection with any of our Universities. Although it is the most recently formed of all the Student Associations connected with the Glasgow University, it is already numerically the second strongest, and intellectually by far the strongest.

Another evidence of the change in Scottish Nationalism to-day is the way in which other people are beginning to realise what is happening. The Labour people in particular are very much rattled. The Labour people realise that at least one of the Scottish National Parties means business. I was asked to stand as Independent Labour Party or Socialist candidate for Banffshire. Some of you may have seen what I replied to the papers. I want to give my reply rather more fully, because it indicates exactly what the attitude of the Scottish National Party is to this sort of thing, and it bears out what Mr. Compton Mackenzie said in his telegram when he said that he and I were rather at one as to the attitude of those who were supporting this National Party in regard to other Parties. What I have said was, "I have been for twenty years a member of the I.L.P. and an active Socialist worker but I am of opinion that the position and prospects of Scotland to-day are so deplorable and ineffective, and action in regard thereto on the part of the present overwhelmingly English legislature so impossible that it behoves all true Scots of whatever Party to sink their other differences in the meantime in the interest of a great national reconstructive movement." (Hear, hear.) To that end I have taken an active part in the formation of the National Party of Scotland, the constitution of which debars its members from standing under any other auspices or assisting the other Parties in any way. It is our intention to contest every Scottish constituency at the next General Election. Steps are now being taken to appoint the necessary candidates. For those of us forming the National Party who have hitherto been Conservatives, Liberals, or Socialists, these English Party political divisions have lost all significance. (Hear, hear.) If our efforts succeed, we will doubtless fall into groups again in course of time, but these will have little or no correspondence to the English political divisions. It is in that spirit and in a spirit of deadly earnestness which I know is being adopted by an ever increasing number of Scots both at home and abroad that I second the Resolution which Mr. Spence proposed. (Applause.)

The resolution was then put to the meeting and carried with only one dissentient.

*Photo: George Outram*

The Duke of Montrose, Compton Mackenzie, R. B. Cunninghame Graham, C.M.G., James Valentine and John MacCormick at the first public meeting of the National Party of Scotland, St Andrew's Halls, Glasgow, 1928.

The formation of the National Party of Scotland was activated by Glasgow University Scottish Nationalist Association headed by John MacCormick, their chairman, and James Valentine, secretary. They conceived the idea of unifying the various parties who were already advocating Scottish Home Rule; the Scottish Home Rule Association, headed by Roland E. Muirhead; the Scots National League, headed by the Hon. Ruaraidh Erskine of Marr and Tom H. Gibson; and the Scottish National Movement, led by Lewis Spence. Their efforts resulted in the formation of the National Party of Scotland in April 1928 and most of the elements involved were represented on the platform of this first big public meeting at the end of 1928 which attracted over three thousand people to the St Andrew's Halls, Glasgow. In April 1934, the National Party of Scotland amalgamated with the Scottish Party to form the Scottish National Party.

D

In 1926 *A Drunk Man Looks at the Thistle* was published and enthusiastically reviewed by Compton Mackenzie. Part of a sequence from *A Drunk Man* reads as follows:

> I micht ha'e been contentit wi' the Rose
> Gin I'd had ony reason to suppose
> That what the English dae can e'er mak' guid
> For what Scots dinna — and first and foremaist should.
>
> I micht ha'e been contentit — gin the feck
> O' my ain folk had grovelled wi less respec',
> But their obsequious devotion
> Made it for me a criminal emotion.
>
> I micht ha'e been contentit — ere I saw
> That there were fields on which it couldna draw,
> (While strang-er roots ran under't) and a'e threid
> O't drew frae Scotland a' that it could need,
> etc., etc.

On 5th November 1929, Compton Mackenzie broadcast an address on B.B.C. Radio entitled "What's Wrong with Scotland?", subtitled "The Soul of the Nation". A large part of this address was transcribed and printed in the December 1929 issue of *The Scots Independent*, the last paragraph headed "Our native culture" reads as follows:

> "Let us see to it that this precious stirring of our consciousness towards the familiar and beloved aspect of our own country is not destroyed by the workaday doubts which will follow soon enough. Let us turn to our own background and forsake utterly the enticement of an alien and for us unnatural culture. We have grafted ourselves upon the rich rose of England. It has flourished on our stock. We have served it well. But the suckers of the wild Scots rose are beginning to show green underneath. Let them grow and blossom, and let the alien graft above, however rich, wither and die. You know our wild Scots rose? it is white, and small, and prickly, and possesses a sharp sweet scent which makes the heart ache."

From these last lines C.M.G. was, it has been suggested, inspired to write the following poem:

### THE LITTLE WHITE ROSE OF SCOTLAND

> The Rose of all the World is not for me,
>                                   I want, for my part,
> Only the little white rose of Scotland
> That smells sharp and sweet — and breaks the heart!

This poem was first published anonymously in *The Modern Scot* in July 1931 "with acknowledgements to Compton Mackenzie" and Compton Mackenzie himself quoted it at the end of a memorable speech at the Bannockburn rally in 1932.

In his autobiography, referring to this occasion, Sir Compton tells how he wound up his speech "with the words Hugh MacDiarmid used in his lyric about the little white rose of Scotland. That lyric has been perhaps the best loved of all he wrote".

On the 5th April 1929, Peggy gave birth to a son they called Walter. Compton Mackenzie and Neil M. Gunn were godfathers.

The wage on *The Montrose Review* was by modern standards low, and in August 1929 C.M.G. was offered the editorship of Compton Mackenzie's radio critical journal, *Vox*. The offer was financially irresistible and, with his wife's encouragement, he accepted, relinquishing the secretaryship of PEN to Helen Cruickshank, as he and the family prepared to move to London.

After only several weeks editing *Vox*, C.M.G. met with a severe accident which put him out of commission for about six weeks. One evening, while travelling home from work upstairs on an open-deck bus, he was rising to leave, when the bus gave a sudden jolt and he was thrown overboard landing on his head on the pavement. He suffered severe concussion and blinding headaches for many months after. He later described the event as "a miraculous escape from death".

Compton Mackenzie rushed to London from Edinburgh and had to arrange for a temporary editor until C.M.G. recovered. However, the magazine was under-capitalised and within a few weeks it had folded and by the time C.M.G. was fit to work he had to find another job.

By this time his marriage to Peggy had started to founder, and when he found work as a public relations officer with an organisation for advancing the interests of Merseyside, they decided to separate; when he arranged to move to Liverpool in 1930 Peggy found work in London and sent the children back to Scotland to live with her mother in Cupar. In 1932 C.M.G. and Peggy were divorced.

In 1939 Christine was on a schoolgirls' trip to Canada when war broke out and she was unable to return. In the summer of 1940 Walter joined his sister in Canada where they were fostered by different families. Christine returned to Scotland in late 1943, married in 1948, and she and her husband emigrated to Canada in 1954. Walter returned to Scotland in 1944 and completed his schooling in Perthshire. He married in 1954 and settled in England.

Peggy emigrated to Canada in 1955, but returned to England a few years later where she married a Canadian, Harry J. Tilar, whom she had met on the Dover ferry. In 1962, she died at Deal in Kent at the age of sixty-five.

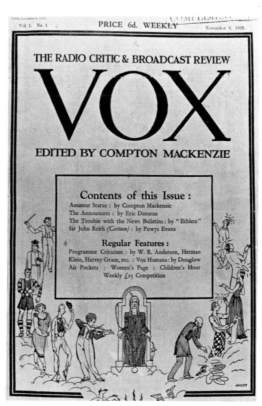

Photo: *Norman Peterkin*

Kaikhosru Shapurji Sorabji outside his home, Corfe Castle, Dorset, 1930s.

**TO MY TWO FRIENDS (E DUOBUS UNUM):**

# HUGH M' DIARMID

## AND

## C. M. GRIEVE

### LIKEWISE

### TO THE EVERLASTING GLORY OF THOSE FEW

### MEN

#### BLESSED AND SANCTIFIED IN THE

#### CURSES AND EXECRATIONS OF THOSE

### MANY

#### WHOSE PRAISE IS ETERNAL DAMNATION

#### JUNE MCMXXX

In 1923, C.M.G. met Kaikhosru Shapurji Sorabji, composer, pianist and critic, in the home of the writer George Reston Malloch in Chingford, Essex.

Sorabji is the son of a Parsi father and a Spanish-Sicilian mother. He has lived most of his life in England.

In the late 1930s Sorabji banned public performance of his music: the only composer known to have done so. In connection with this self-imposed veto, he has issued the following statement: "I am not a 'modern' composer in the inverted commas sense. I utterly and indignantly repudiate the epithet as being in any way applicable to me. I write very long, very elaborate works that are entirely alien and antipathetic to the fashionable tendencies promoted, publicised and plugged by the various 'establishments' revolving around this or that modern composer. Why do I neither seek nor encourage performance of my works? Because they are neither intended for, nor suitable for it under present, or indeed any foreseeable conditions: no performance at all is vastly preferable to an obscene travesty."

In 1930 Sorabji published his *Opus Clavicembalisticum* for piano solo. The Latin title literally means "Keyboardistic Work". The opus which plays for two-and-a-half hours with two brief intermissions, was premiered by Sorabji in Glasgow in 1930 and is dedicated in the published score "To my two friends, Hugh MacDiarmid and C. M. Grieve".

In 1962 Sorabji composed a "footnote-in-music" to the *Opus Clavicembalisticum*: a short though complex piano piece entitled *Fantasiattina sul nome illustre dell' egregio poeta Christopher Grieve ossia Hugh MacDiarmid* (Little Fantasy on the musical monogram, the illustrious name of the distinguished poet Christopher Grieve or Hugh MacDiarmid).

There is a chapter on Sorabji in MacDiarmid's second volume of autobiography, *The Company I've Kept*; being the transcript of a tape-recorded, all-night *conversazione* between C.M.G., the pianist John Ogden and the pianist/composer Ronald Stevenson.

In 1976 Sorabji lifted his veto on the performance of his work.

Photo: H. Scott Harrison

On his return from Liverpool in 1931, Helen B. Cruickshank held a party for C.M.G. at her home in Corstorphine, Edinburgh. Pictured left to right are — Mrs Cruickshank, C.M.G., Anne MacDiarmid, John Rafferty, Mrs Thomas Henderson, Prof. Otto Schlapp, F. Marian McNeill, N. Jamieson, John Tonge, Peter Taylor, J. H. Whyte, W. D. MacColl, Helen B. Cruickshank, Mr William Burt and, in front, Nannie K. Wells.

## THE EEMIS STANE

I' the how-dumb-deid o' the cauld hairst nicht
The warl' like an eemis stane
Wags i' the lift;
An' my eerie memories fa'
    Like a yowdendrift.

Like a yowdendrift so's I couldna read
The words cut oot i' the stane
Had the fug o' fame
An' history's hazelraw
No' yirdit thaim.

In 1931 C.M.G. met Valda Trevlyn in Hennekey's Bar, High Holborn, London. The bar was a centre for literary meetings and Valda was taken there by a boyfriend and eventually introduced to C.M.G. She doesn't remember C.M.G. taking much notice of her although every time she produced a cigarette his hand would appear with a light. Valda's friend wanted them to become engaged but she decided against it. A relationship developed with C.M.G., who had recently parted from Peggy, and after a while they left London and went to live together at a friend's cottage, "Cootes", in Thakeham, Surrey. They lived there for six months and on 28th July 1932 Valda gave birth to Michael at Steyning Hospital near Thakeham.

A crayon drawing of C.M.G. by "Æ" (George William Russell) used as a frontispiece for *First Hymn to Lenin and Other Poems*, 1931.

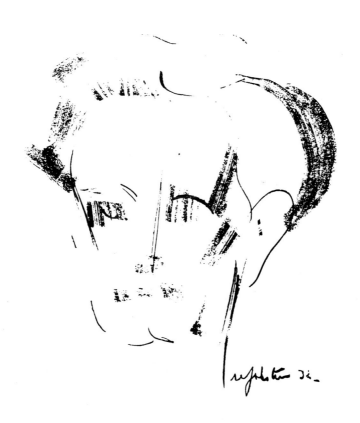

Drawing by William Johnstone, used as the frontispiece for *Second Hymn to Lenin*, published by Valda Trevlyn, 1932.

The village of Thakeham with the White Lion pub on the right-hand side of the street. During a convivial evening here C.M.G. was inspired to write and Valda produced the only paper available from the ladies' toilet. In a matter of minutes C.M.G. wrote the poem "Milk-Wort and Bog-Cotton". During his stay in Thakeham C.M.G. also wrote "Water Music", "Tarras" and "Second Hymn to Lenin".

## MILK-WORT AND BOG COTTON

### To Seumas O'Sullivan

Cwa'een like milk-wort and bog-cotton hair!
I love you, earth, in this mood best o' a'
When the shy spirit like a laich wind moves
And frae the lift nae shadow can fa'
Since there's nocht left to thraw a shadow there
Owre een like milk-wort and milk-white cotton hair.

Wad that nae leaf upon anither wheeled
A shadow either and nae root need dern
In sacrifice to let sic beauty be!
But deep surroondin' darkness I discern
Is aye the price o' licht. Wad licht revealed
Naething but you, and nicht nocht else concealed.

A picnic in Dr Stanley Robertson's garden in Musselburgh, 1932. Left to right—C.M.G., Mrs Robertson, Robin Black, Mrs Black and Dr Robertson.

After six months in Thakeham with very little income from his writing, C.M.G. and his family were forced to return to Edinburgh where they lived for several weeks with Robin Black, a journalist friend, at his home in Portobello, Edinburgh. Robin Black published a weekly magazine, *The Free Man*, with the financial backing of Dr Stanley Robertson, a prosperous dental surgeon from Musselburgh. The magazine propagated the Douglas Social Credit scheme and Scottish Nationalism. When C.M.G. was offered the post of editor, with a wage of £2 per week, he accepted.

Reasonable accommodation was always hard to find, but eventually C.M.G. was able to rent an old cottage outside Longniddry, near Edinburgh, where the family lived for about one year.

This was an extremely desperate financial period. After the weekly rent of ten shillings was paid, the remainder of his income was spent on food, drink and bus fares to Edinburgh.

Soon they decided to take rented accommodation back in Edinburgh, but the situation failed to improve.

At this time C.M.G. was corresponding with Dr David Orr who had a medical practice on the Shetland island of Whalsay, and when Dr Orr invited him to visit, he was pleased to accept and travelled north in 1933.

C.M.G., Valda and Michael, shortly áfter their arrival on Whalsay.

On board the Leith to Lerwick steamer after leaving hospital.

Visiting Whalsay, C.M.G. could see the prospects of a more economic existence. Accommodation was cheap, and the main diet of mutton, fish and vegetables was sufficient. The relative solitude of island life also appealed to him and after an introduction to a local landowner, he was offered the rental of a cottage at 27/6 per annum with the inclusion of "peat leave", the right to cut peat from the surrounds. Water had to be fetched from a well at some distance, but with free fuel and cheap accommodation, it promised an easier life than Edinburgh. C.M.G. sent for his family and they joined him within a few weeks.

In 1933, C.M.G. was expelled from the South Edinburgh branch of the National Party of Scotland for Communism. His application for reinstatement was rejected by the council of the N.P.S.

In 1934, C.M.G. joined the Communist Party of Great Britain.

On 11th April 1934, C.M.G.'s mother died at Waterbeck, near Langholm, at the age of seventy-seven and was buried beside her husband in Langholm cemetery.

In the spring of 1934, in Rutherford's Bar, South Bridge, Edinburgh, C.M.G. was introduced to the Gaelic poet, Sorley MacLean by George Davie; the start of a long and lasting friendship.

In 1934, C.M.G. was involved in a plan to retrieve the Stone of Destiny from Westminster Abbey in London, the idea being to return it to Scotland and dispose of it in a deep river or loch. The stone displayed in Westminster Abbey was known to be a fake and the action was simply to eradicate another act of English domination. C.M.G. travelled to London but the plan was abandoned when security proved to be insurmountable.

In August 1935, Sorley MacLean spent a week with C.M.G. in Whalsay but C.M.G. was far from well. The accumulated stress of the breakdown of his first marriage and the fight to survive as a writer with little financial income had taken their toll. His body weight had reduced drastically, and in September the inevitable nervous breakdown occurred. Francis George Scott heard about his condition and arranged with Dr Orr to have him admitted to Murray Royal Hospital, Perth, at his expense, where he would be assured of first-class attention.

After seven weeks in Perth, C.M.G. recovered sufficiently, and in a weak condition was allowed to return to Whalsay.

Prior to this breakdown C.M.G. is seen wearing jacket and trousers. After his return from hospital he decided the kilt would be healthier attire and he is seen in the Murray tartan.

" Come a' you nit-wits, knaves and fools. . . . ."

From *The Scots Observer*, 7th January 1933.

The jacket wrapper of *Scottish Scene.* A joint work of C.M.G. and Lewis Grassic Gibbon, published in 1934.

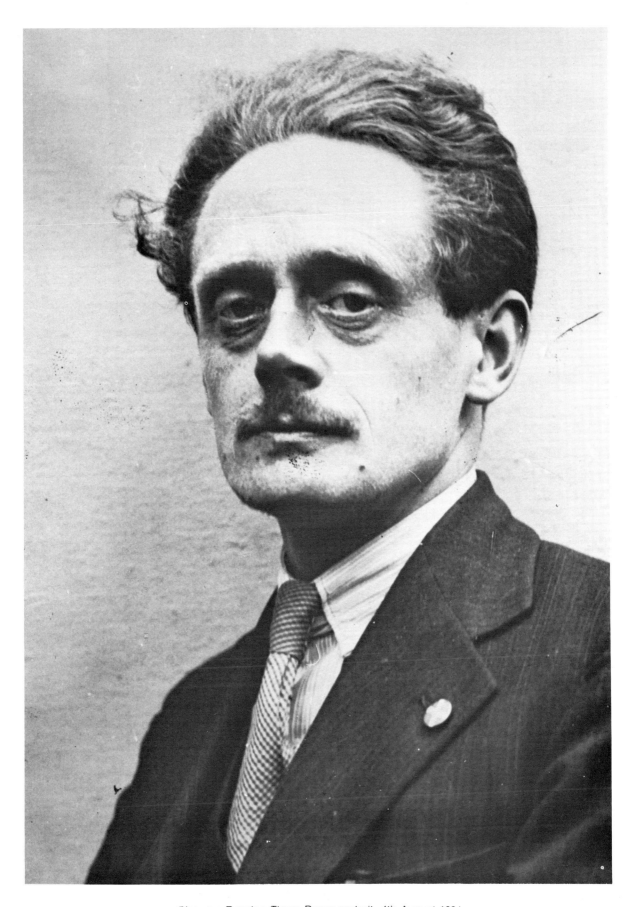

*Glasgow Evening Times* Press portrait, 4th August 1934.

JOIN THE

# HUGH MACDIARMID BOOK CLUB

Organised to secure publication for a constant stream of revolutionary Scottish Literature, devoted to anti-English separatism.

The majority of the entire Scottish electorate votes for the Left, but this is not only nullified in practice by the English connection but is so far almost entirely unreflected in journalism and publishing. Mr. MacDiarmid's aim is the establishment of a Scottish Workers' Autonymous Communist Republic and a revival of literature in the distinctive Scottish tradition.

SEND NO MONEY, but sign this form and post it to the Secretary, Hugh MacDiarmid Book Club, Whalsay, via Lerwick, Shetland Islands :—

I agree for one year from this date to accept on publication the four or five books to be issued during the ensuing twelve months, at preferential rates to Club members, by the Hugh MacDiarmid Book Club, also the weekly paper, *Red Scotland,* and the monthly *Hammer and Thistle,* at a total inclusive rate, including postage, of 40/- [books to be paid for on delivery, and the *Red Scotland* and *Hammer and Thistle* annual subscriptions (10/- each) on receipt of the first issues of these.]

*Name* ...........................................................................

*Address* ...................................     ...................................

...................................     *Date*...................

(*Please fill in in clear block letters.*)

## HUGH MACDIARMID'S BOOKS INCLUDE:—

*Poetry*: A Drunk Man looks at the Thistle; Selected Poems; Stony Limits; First Hymn to Lenin; Second Hymn to Lenin, etc., etc.

*Criticism*: At the Sign of the Thistle; Contemporary Scottish Studies; Scottish Scene, etc., etc.

*Biography*: Scottish Eccentrics, etc., etc.

*Fiction*: Annals of the Five Senses; Five Bits of Millar, etc., etc.

*Politics*: Albyn, or Scotland and the Future, etc., etc.

*Music*: The Present Condition of Scottish Music.

*Agriculture*: Rural Reform (with Lord Passfield and others.)

(Thirty titles in all.)

Early Club issues will include *Cornish Heroic Song for Valda Trevlyn* and *The Red Lion* (a poetical gallimaufry of the Glasgow slums). Further Club news in *Red Scotland* weekly.

SCOTLAND'S VORTEX-MAKER

C.M. GRIEVE

Caricature by Coia from *The Bookman*, September 1934.

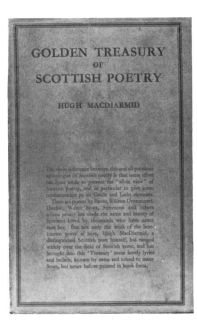

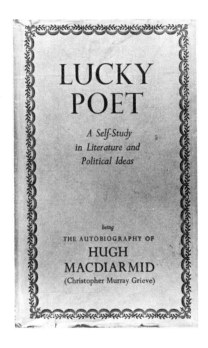

With plenty of fresh air from sailing with the local fishermen and settling down once again to his writing, his health improved.

During the years in Whalsay, C.M.G. co-authored *Scottish Scene* with Lewis Grassic Gibbon, wrote *Scottish Eccentrics*, *The Islands of Scotland*, edited *The Golden Treasury of Scottish Poetry*, founded the literary magazine *The Voice of Scotland* and in 1939 completed his autobiography, *Lucky Poet*, a massive undertaking of one-quarter million words written long-hand in a concentrated period working seven days and nights with very little sleep. The final publication (1943) contained only a quarter of the original manuscript.

Income was largely from his publisher's advances (usually £50) received on the acceptance of a manuscript. Between times the local grocer allowed extended credit until the next advance arrived. There was also the occasional trip to Aberdeen to broadcast for the B.B.C. which could be extended to visit friends in Edinburgh and keep in touch with the Scottish literary scene.

Above left—C.M.G. relaxing in his study room.
Above right—Valda and Michael, aged two.
Opposite top left—George Davie, Mrs Croskey and C.M.G. during Davie's
six-week visit in the summer of 1937.
Opposite top right—C.M.G. at the well.
Opposite left—Michael, age five, photographed in Lerwick.
Opposite right—Drawing by Barbara Niven during a visit to Whalsay in 1939.

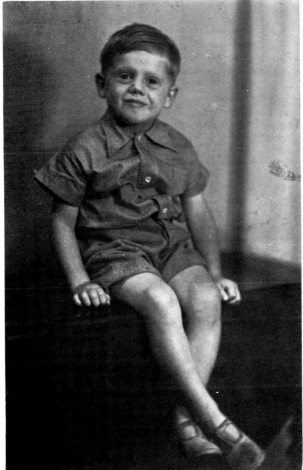

65

Photographs taken by Helen B. Cruickshank in Princes Street Gardens during C.M.G.'s visit to Edinburgh in May 1936. C.M.G. was living in Whalsay and had travelled to Aberdeen to broadcast for the B.B.C. He then visited Edinburgh and stayed with Tom and Mary MacDonald at their home in West Claremont Street for two weeks.

Opposite top left—C.M.G. and Helen B. Cruickshank. Bottom left—C.M.G. with Mary and Tom MacDonald (Fionn Mac Colla). Bottom right—C.M.G., Valda and Michael at the door of "Dinnieduff", Helen B. Cruickshank's residence in Corstorphine.

C.M.G. and Francis George Scott the composer, who was formerly his primary teacher at Langholm Academy and subsequently lecturer in music at Jordanhill Training College, Glasgow.

The collaboration between these two Borderers (Scott was from Hawick) must be unique in literary and musical history. They were on the same wavelength to a very remarkable degree. Scott's song settings were published in five volumes by Bayley and Ferguson, Glasgow, from 1922-1939, entitled *Scottish Lyrics Set to Music by Francis George Scott*. Volume three included settings of MacDiarmid's "Wheesht Wheesht", "The Eemis Stane", "Crowdieknowe", "Moonstruck", "Love", "Milk-Wort and Bog-Cotton" and "An Apprentice Angel". Volume five included "The Love Sick Lass", "Empty Vessel" and "The Watergaw". There was a subsequent volume of later settings, *Thirty-five Scottish Lyrics and Other Poems*, published by Bayley and Ferguson for the Saltire Society, Edinburgh, in 1949, and this volume included settings of MacDiarmid's "Country Life", "First Love", "Hungry Waters", "I Wha Aince in Heaven's Heicht", "The Innumerable Christ", "Lourd on my Hert", "The Man in the Moon", "The Sauchs in the Reuch Heuch Hauch" and "Sunny Gale".

*Seven Songs for Baritone Voice* by Francis George Scott was also published by Bayley and Ferguson and included "Reid Een" by MacDiarmid.

C.M.G. dedicated four of his books to Scott, and in 1955 had published *Francis George Scott: an essay on the occasion of his seventy-fifth birthday, 25th January 1955*, by Hugh MacDiarmid, M. Macdonald.

Francis George Scott received an honorary doctorate from Glasgow University in 1957 in recognition of his musical achievement. He died in November 1958 at the age of seventy-eight.

"The Scottish Renaissance", by William Johnstone, 1934, depicting MacDiarmid and spirits rising from their graves, intended to indicate stirrings of new life in Scotland.

Line illustration by William Johnstone, reproduced on the jacket of
*Second Hymn to Lenin and other Poems*, 1935.

## WHEESHT, WHEESHT

Wheesht, wheesht, my foolish hert,
For weel ye ken
I widna ha'e ye stert
Auld ploys again.

It's guid to see her lie
Sae snod an' cool,
A' lust o' lovin' by—
Wheesht, wheesht, ye fule!

# VOTE FOR GRIEVE—HE'S GOT GUTS

## Vote for Grieve
## Honour Yourself
## Show Your Courage
## Make History

Addressing the students of Aberdeen University in his stand for the rectorship in 1933.

ABERDEEN UNIVERSITY
RECTORIAL ELECTION, 1933

| | |
|---|---|
| Rt. Hon. Walter E. Elliot, M.P. | 307 |
| G. K. Chesterton | 220 |
| C. M. Grieve | 158 |
| Aldous Huxley | 117 |

RECTOR—Rt. Hon. Walter E. Elliot, M.P.

EDINBURGH UNIVERSITY
RECTORIAL ELECTION, 1935

| | |
|---|---|
| Viscount Allenby | 825 |
| Dr Douglas Chalmers Watson | 792 |
| Lord Clydesdale | 292 |
| C. M. Grieve | 88 |

RECTOR—Viscount Allenby

EDINBURGH UNIVERSITY
RECTORIAL ELECTION, 1936

| | |
|---|---|
| Dr J. Donald Pollock | 795 |
| Sir Herbert Grierson | 664 |
| Dr Douglas Chalmers Watson | 571 |
| C. M. Grieve | 266 |
| Rt. Hon. Lord Salveson | 134 |

RECTOR—Sir Herbert Grierson

The Aberdeen rectorial election was carried out on a system which involved the four University Nations voting within themselves and then combining the results. The Edinburgh elections were held on the single transferable vote system. The figures given here are the results of the first count.

Lord Allenby, who was elected Rector of Edinburgh University in 1935, died shortly after, hence the early election in 1936.

A watercolour by Jessie Kocmanova, 1936. Inspired by MacDiarmid's poem, *A Drunk Man Looks at the Thistle.*

*Photo: Charles Nicol*

C.M.G. at work in the copper shell band department of Mechan's Engineering Co.

At the outbreak of war in 1939, C.M.G. and his family were still living in Whalsay. Eventually, in January 1941, C.M.G. was conscripted for national service and reported to Glasgow, leaving Valda and Michael on the island. There was the possibility of manual labour on the roads, but Helen B. Cruickshank, who was employed in the Civil Service, was able to arrange for him to be allocated engineering work as he was still suffering from the effects of his breakdown and physically unfit for heavy work.

Francis George Scott and his family were living in Glasgow at the time, and C.M.G. stayed with them at their home in Munro Road while he completed a six-month government training course and qualified as a precision fitter. He was then employed in the copper shell band department of Mechan's Engineering Company, Scotstoun, Glasgow, which specialised in the production of war materials.

After he had worked in Glasgow for a year, Valda and Michael were able to join him and after a few weeks living with friends, they found furnished accommodation at 35 Havelock Street.

The Wallace Day Rally at Elderslie, Renfrewshire, 22nd August 1942. Organised by the Scottish National Party to commemorate the life of Sir William Wallace, the great Scottish patriot, born there in 1270 A.D. Left to right—Arthur Donaldson, Robert McIntyre, Alex Sloan, M.P., Matt Ferguson, R. E. Muirhead, Oliver Brown and C.M.G.

## THE LOVE-SICK LASS

As white's the blossom on the rise
The wee lass was
That 'bune the green risp i' the fu' mune
Cannily blaws.

Sweet as the cushie's croud she sang
Wi'r wee reid mou'—
Wha sauch-like i' the lowe o' luve
Lies sabbin' noo!

SCOTS MAKARS
CALENDARS

Selections from the works of
HUGH MACDIARMID

[Photo by Nicol, Glasgow.

...ght

...for aye
...nna win free
...haud it fast
...me,

...ince mair
...eside
...it's gane
...clutch 'll bide

...irl
...strike back,
...tin' o' love
...lk

**1945**

| | |
|---|---|
| 21 | 28 |
| 22 | 29 |
| 23 | 30 |
| 24 | 31 |
| 25 | |
| 26 | |
| 27 | |

Scots Makars Calendars for 1945, published by Robin McKelvie Black. This carried one of C.M.G.'s poems for each month of the year.

Left to right—William Maclellan, Douglas Young, C.M.G., George Arnot, Maurice Lindsay and George Bruce at a poetry reading in Glasgow under the auspices of The Dunedin Society, 1947.

C.M.G. enjoyed living in Glasgow although there was little time for him to write, leaving home in the early hours of the morning with compulsory overtime every night.

In 1943 he was transferred to the Merchant Service as first engineer on a Norwegian vessel, H.M.V. *Gurli*, based at Greenock, servicing British and American men-of-war in the estuaries of the River Clyde.

At the General Election of 1945, C.M.G. stood for Kelvingrove as an Independent Scottish Nationalist but only received 4.9 per cent of the vote and lost his deposit.

When the war ended in 1945 C.M.G. was made redundant and registered as unemployed in Glasgow.

The years of the depression following the Second World War made life extremely difficult for C.M.G. and his family. Valda found work as a bookshop assistant with John Smith and Son, St Vincent Street, earning £2 per week, but it was impossible for C.M.G. to find regular work and he was mostly registered as unemployed, apart from the Christmas period when the G.P.O. engaged extra staff and he was employed to sort mail; and a brief spell in 1945 when he worked as a staff reporter for *The Carlisle Journal*. From Havelock Street they moved to similar accommodation at 27 Arundel Drive and later to a basement flat in Victoria Park Crescent.

# Scottish National Party
## KELVINGROVE
# ELECTION MEETING

in the

## COSMO CINEMA, Rose St.
## SUNDAY, 10th JUNE, 1945
### AT 6-30 P.M.

*Speaker:*

Mr. C. M. GRIEVE, Kelvingrove

*Supported by:*

Mr. DOUGLAS YOUNG
Mr. R. B. WILKIE
Mr. W. OLIVER BROWN

*Chairman* - - Mr. P. J. CONNELLY

# VOTE *for* GRIEVE
# *and a* Square Deal
# *for* SCOTLAND

Published by P. J. Connelly, 647 Argyle Street, Glasgow
Printed by John S. Burns & Sons, 195 Buccleuch Street, Glasgow, C.3

The heading on this election poster is incorrect. C.M.G. was not a member of the S.N.P. at this time but was standing as an Independent Scottish Nationalist and Republican. His election agent, Mr P. J. Connelly, was a member of the S.N.P. and responsible for the poster.

GENERAL ELECTION, 14th July 1945 (Kelvingrove)

| | |
|---|---|
| J. L. Williams (Lab.) | 12,273 |
| Rt. Hon. Walter Elliot (Con.) | 12,185 |
| C. M. Grieve (Ind. Scot. Nat.) | 1,314 |
| Capt. C. J. E. Morgan (Lib.) | 919 |

Caricature of Hugh MacDiarmid by Sydney Goodsir Smith drawn in Sorley MacLean's flat in Queen Street, Edinburgh, in 1948.

# C.M.G. — PERPETUAL OPPOSITION*

## I

The guid conceit o rebellie men
Is in their faith alane
No in the richt o the cause ava
For yon aye ends the same
—Tyrants up and beggars doun
As you and I weill ken.

But it's the traist in betterment
The will to sort the ills
Kennan the treason at the end
As we ken ower weill
—Tyrants they and beggars we
As is and was and aye sall be.

Here I stand, auld Chris, wi ye:
As man is ne'er perfectible
The anerlie role for a bard can be
Oppositioun perpetual
—And tyrants whiles may feel the smairt
O' the sang unsung i' the beggar's hairt.

Richt freedom's surelie follie's dream
But reason's no the bard's concern
I'm for the faith wad shift our beam
And the mote i' the ee o the unborn bairn:
Divine discontent alane
Can justifie God's weys til men
—Tho beggars walk and tyrants ride
In beggars' hairts find freemen's pride!
     —*Mebbe!*

* Whether I read this pregnant thocht in ane of his works or heard the bard tell it in conversation I canna just richtlie mynd; for all that, it's an *immortal* or evergreen in Hugh MacDiarmid's life and work. Mair's the pitie, neither he nor I can track it doun til a richt context — but it byles doun til this: MacDiarmid is a dour and unregenerate Scots Republican, but (says his theorie) gin siccan government wan throu til the seats of the michtie the morn's morn, his sel wad be the firstmaist gangan intil opposition.

Sydney Goodsir Smith

Sydney Goodsir Smith and C.M.G. in conference, the Café Royal Bar, Edinburgh, January 1948. The Café Royal Bar was more spacious and quieter than The Abbotsford or Milne's Bar, and it was here that C.M.G. would meet his friends when a matter required serious discussion.

*Photo: Evening Times*

Left to right: Douglas Young, C.M.G. and Eoin O'Mahoney, speaking at a meeting in Glasgow in support of Robert Blair Wilkie, the Independent Nationalist candidate in the Camlachie by-election, 23rd December 1949.

Left to right—Calum Campbell of the Caledonian Press, Glasgow, which published the nationalist newspaper *The National Weekly*, Hamish Henderson, Marion and Morris Blythman, C.M.G. and Archie Meikle, at Willie Kellock's home in Bo'ness after a St Andrew's night ceilidh, 25th November 1949.

During his stay in Glasgow, C.M.G. edited *The National Weekly* in support of the Nationalist cause. He also wrote the front page and most of the literary content.

F

Left to right—Sorley MacLean, Alexander Scott, Sydney Goodsir Smith and C.M.G., photographed in North St David Street, Edinburgh, 10th February 1948, after recording a poetry reading at the B.B.C. in Queen Street for Swedish radio producer Torsten Jungstedt. This was later broadcast by the B.B.C. Overseas Service to Sweden.

C.M.G. with Sorley MacLean, the Gaelic poet, and Hector MacIver, then principal teacher of English at Edinburgh Royal High School. MacIver was also a well-known broadcaster and Gaelic playwright, 1949.

*Photo: Edinburgh Evening Dispatch*

Sydney Goodsir Smith, Madame Elistratova, Russian teacher of English literature, C.M.G., Boris Polevoi, Russian novelist, Professor Samuel Marshak, Russian translator of Robert Burns, and publisher William MacLellan, at a gathering in Edinburgh under the auspices of the Scottish-U.S.S.R. Friendship Society in 1950.

# Scots Republican accepts King's pension

C. M. GRIEVE (Hugh MacDiarmid), 50-year-old Scottish poet and Republican, who owes no allegiance to the Crown, has been granted a Civil List pension of £150 a year by the King.

Mr Attlee recommended the award for "great services to British literature".

After receiving the first cheque Mr Grieve said last night:—

*"I was very glad to accept Mr Attlee's offer of the pension even though I am a Republican and it is a Royal grant.*

"I refused to sign the Scottish Covenant because for one thing it meant giving allegiance to the Throne, and secondly, I am a separatist and the Covenant calls for 'Ulster-model' Home Rule, while I prefer complete independence for Scotland.

"At any rate I shall be glad of the £150 a year because poetry is in the doldrums today and a man like me, primarily a poet, finds it difficult to make a living."

Called "the father of the Scottish literary renaissance" and by some critics "a hater of all things English", Grieve is a fervid Republican.

He received news of the award in his cottage home in the grounds of the Duke of Hamilton's estate near Strathaven.

**Footnote:** Civil List pensions are granted to "such persons only as have just claims on the Royal beneficence, or who by their personal services to the Crown, or by their performance of duties to the public, or by their useful discoveries in science and attainments in literature and the arts have merited the gracious consideration of their Sovereign and the gratitude of their country." — Act of Parliament in the reign of Queen Victoria.

*Scottish Daily Express* report.

On a week's cultural visit to Moscow in 1950 with members of the Scottish-U.S.S.R. Friendship Society. Pictured outside the Moscow Municipal Council Building, the party includes fifth from left, Prof. Charles Wrenn, sixth Andrew Rothstein, tenth Rev. Etienne Watts, thirteenth C.M.G. and fourteenth Leslie Hurry.

*Photo: The Glasgow Herald*

C.M.G., David Campbell, president of the Scottish-U.S.S.R. Friendship Society, and George Hamilton.

Photo: *The Glasgow Herald*

C.M.G. with 18-year-old poet-friend Arnold Wesker of London, outside Dungavel House in 1950.

In 1950, through their association in the Saltire Society, the Earl of Selkirk introduced C.M.G. to his brother, the Duke of Hamilton, who offered him a five-apartment outhouse at his home, Dungavel House, near Strathaven, Lanarkshire.

C.M.G. and his family moved in but after barely a year the entire property was bought by the National Coal Board to be converted into a resident training centre for young miners and they were asked to leave.

GENERAL ELECTION, 23rd Feb. 1950 (Kelvingrove)

| | |
|---|---|
| Rt. Hon. Walter Elliot (Con.) | 15,197 |
| J. L. Williams (Lab.) | 13,973 |
| S. J. Ranger (Lib.) | 831 |
| C. M. Grieve (Ind. Scot. Nat.) | 639 |

85

# Kelvingrove Election-1950

## Christopher Murray
# GRIEVE

### INDEPENDENT
### SCOTTISH NATIONALIST
### CANDIDATE

*To the Electors*:—

"WE'LL VOTE FOR OURSELVES THIS TIME":—A woman in Argyle Street told me the other day: "You needn't be afraid. We'll vote for ourselves this time. We'll vote for Scotland." I hope and believe the majority of the Kelvingrove electors are of the same mind. There is much need.

I have devoted myself to the Scottish Nationalist Movement, cultural and political, for over thirty years. I have always believed and said that the vast majority of Scottish people would vote for Scottish Self-Government if and when the Scottish case was put frankly and fully before them. I am accordingly not surprised that nearly a million Scots (one in five of our population) have already signed the Covenant. The Covenant, however, does not go nearly far enough. It is merely the thin end of the wedge. Even so if the Scottish electorate had been given the chance of voting for Covenant candidates I am certain they would have swept the country. Instead of that, most Scottish voters have only Labour and Tory candidates in their constituencies — and both the Labour and Tory Parties are English-controlled and anti-Covenant.

THE CASE FOR SCOTTISH INDEPENDENCE:—

The case for Scottish Independence was put long ago by Robert Burns when he wrote:— "What are the boasted advantages which my country has gained from this Union with England that can counter-balance the annihilation of her independence and her very name? "

ENGLAND WILL DRAG US DOWN:—

The answer is none, but very much the other way. Unless we sever the connection England will drag us down in her own ruin. Scotland and England cannot be treated as a "single economic unit." They stand at opposite economic poles. Scotland is a self-supporting, food-exporting country which, if independent, would have a favourable trade balance and be able to pay for all it needs to import out of its exports. Scotland is also grossly underpopulated and according to Lord Boyd Orr could—and should — maintain three times its present population. England is in the opposite case and cannot and never could support 40 million people. It is now generally agreed that England will have to part with about one-third of her population. This does not mean that Scotland should not help England in her crisis — but it should be left to the free will of the Scottish people, not simply taken for granted and above all not done to the detriment of our own vital interests as at present.

SCOTLAND'S GREAT RESOURCES.—Scottish resources of all kinds—crops, stock, minerals, fisheries—stand in relation to English resources proportionately to population in the ratio of three to one. Why then is Scotland so much worse off than England? Why are Scottish wages so much lower? Why in times of crisis is Scottish unemployment 50 per cent. greater? Why is Scottish housing six times worse than English? Why are Scottish slums the worst in Europe? It is not because Scots people are poorer in industry and initiative. They are famous all over the world for these very qualities. What intervenes to prevent them applying their abilities successfully in their own country? There can only be one answer—our relations with England. The disparity between Scotland and England can only be accounted for by the unfair treatment of Scotland and the systematic sacrifice of Scottish interests to English interests all along the line by the predominantly English government at Westminster. It does not matter what political party is in power.

## LABOUR HAS BETRAYED SCOTLAND'S CAUSE:—

The Labour Party has betrayed the Scottish cause. Until less than five years ago it always had Scottish Home Rule as one of its planks. All the great pioneers of the Labour Party were Scottish Home Rulers. But what is the position under a Labour government to-day?

Mr. Attlee gave a personal promise in 1945 that a Labour government would establish a Scottish Parliament—but he set no time limit. We cannot wait any longer. Investigation has shown that in many parts of Scotland 80 per cent. of the adult population are in favour of Scottish Self-Government, and the operative word is **NOW!**

Increasing consideration of Scottish affairs has led to the great mass movement of the Scottish people behind the Covenant. Even in the nationalised coal industry, the Scottish miners cannot go to the Scottish Coal Board to have their wages raised to the level of the English miners. All the power is retained by the National Coal Board.

Scotland is the only country in the world that hasn't had the opportunity of developing dock accommodation in relation to its capacity for building ships. Scotland builds the biggest and grandest ships that sail the seas, but we cannot berth them. They have to find a home down South.

Scotland is the only country in the world with a great engineering tradition and a world-recognised high standard of engineering that has no aircraft industry.

Scotland has no motor car industry, although that industry had its start in Scotland.

Scottish agriculture has never received the attention it is entitled to. If one-third of the £15 million granted to increase livestock in Queensland were granted to the Highlands they could produce more in five years than Queensland will in twenty.

## NO POLITICAL PARTY

I belong to no political party, but believe that in Scotland the Scottish cause should come first and foremost all the time, and I ask for your support on these grounds.

I do not want any mere administrative adjustment. I want a Scottish Parliament so that Scotland can make her independent voice heard in world affairs again, and, above all, in the paramount questions of War and Peace, foreign affairs, and finance.

*Mr. Grieve, under his pen-name of Hugh MacDiarmid, is internationally famous as the greatest living Scottish poet and true successor of Robert Burns. An American critic, Kenneth Rexroth, recently said: "He is undoubtedly one of the most important writers in Great Britain to-day and a genuine world literary figure." All his leading fellow-writers in Scotland, and in other European countries, have twice presented him with public testimonials in token of his great services to Scottish life and letters during the past thirty years.*

Printed by John S. Burns & Sons, Glasgow, C.3., and
Published by John Goldie, Election Agent, 55 Bath Street, Glasgow.

Through William MacLellan, the publisher, and his wife, C.M.G. was introduced to Mr Tweedie, a Lanarkshire farmer, who agreed to rent the farm cottage called Brownsbank near Biggar. There were no modern conveniences, the toilet was outside, water was carried from a tap in the garden and the two rooms were illuminated at night by oil lamps, but at least it was somewhere to live and in January 1951 the family moved in.

Photo: The Scotsman

Left to right—Mrs Foggie, Albert Mackie, Douglas Young, C.M.G. and Valda at the presentation of the portrait by David Foggie, R.S.A., to C.M.G. by his friends and admirers, the Scotia Hotel, Edinburgh, 28th August 1951. The portrait was completed in Edinburgh shortly before C.M.G. left for Whalsay in 1933.

# PORTRAIT OF A MAKAR

### Tribute to "Hugh MacDiarmid"

A portrait of C. M. Grieve ("Hugh MacDiarmid") was, on Saturday, at a luncheon given by his friends and admirers in the Scotia Hotel, Edinburgh, handed over to the poet by the chairman, Mr Albert Mackie. The portrait was a drawing by the late David Foggie, R.S.A., exhibited at the recent Royal Scottish Academy exhibition in Edinburgh, and purchased by a group of younger writers in Scots.

Notable personalities in Scottish literature, as well as representatives of several countries, were at the gathering, which was the occasion for tributes to the work of Hugh MacDiarmid. Among those present were Dr O. H. Mavor ("James Bridie"), Mr Eric Linklater, Mr Neil Gunn, Mr William Power, Mr Ivor Brown, Mr Francis George Scott, Mr Benno Schotz, M. Joseph Chiari, M. Pierre Emmanuel, Mr Andrew Tannahill, a descendant of the poet Tannahill, Mrs Grieve, and Mrs Foggie.

In a tribute to Hugh MacDiarmid, read at the luncheon, Mr T. S. Eliot wrote: "Hugh MacDiarmid's refusal to become merely another successful English poet, and his pursuing a course which, at first, some of his admirers deplored and some of his detractors derided, has had important consequences and has justified itself. It will eventually be admitted that he has done more also for English poetry, by committing some of his finest verse to Scots, than if he had elected to write exclusively in the Southern dialect."

Mr Mackie and Mr Grieve spoke in Scots.

Mr Mackie said that what MacDiarmid had done for the language and its poetry was little more than symbolic of his real work. A great contribution had been his criticism and cry to us to waken up as a nation and not to be content with petty achievements. In his critical work he had stirred up the alert and active, inquisitive and ambitious Scotland we saw today.

Mr Grieve, in his reply, said: "Our greatest enemy is the educational system. . . . To be a scriever it's necessar to jeuk the deid weight o' education at a' costs, and aboon a', sic a man has to remain an independent human being, and tak' care no to acquire ony o' the usual cunning, timid deference to men o' established reputation."

Expressing pleasure at so many of his friends being present, he paid a tribute to his old Edinburgh schoolmaster, Mr George Ogilvie.

"The Scottish movement," said Mr Grieve, "is well under wey among the mass o' oor fowk, but it is nae channelled yit to ony particular organisation. The condition o' Scotland today ca's for a' the bitterness we can possibly distil."

*Edinburgh Evening Dispatch* report.

*Photo: The Hamilton Advertiser*

Mrs Valda Grieve and Mrs Adala Murray being escorted by police from an open air meeting at Strathaven after throwing eggs at Emmanuel Shinwell, M.P., then War Minister. Shinwell had been a conscientious objector during the First World War and refused Michael Grieve any support in his appeal.

*Photo: The Scottish Sunday Express*

Left to right—R. E. Muirhead, Michael Grieve and C.M.G. at the gate of Saughton Prison, Edinburgh, on Michael's release.

In June 1952, after a lengthy legal battle that had lasted several years, Michael Grieve was sentenced at Glasgow Sheriff Court to six months' imprisonment.

Back in December 1950, the Edinburgh Appellate Tribunal had rejected his application to be registered as a conscientious objector on grounds which included a deep-rooted abhorrence to the imperial war being waged against Kenya; and on the belief that conscription was a violation of the Act of Union which safeguarded Scots from being sent overseas by a Westminster Parliament. The chairman of the tribunal commented: "If he (Michael) had been at Bannockburn I do not believe he would have been a camp follower." The jail sentence was served in Barlinnie Prison, Glasgow, and Saughton Prison, Edinburgh.

Photo: The Glasgow Herald

Left to right—C.M.G., Hugh Paterson, Wendy Wood, Matt Somerville, Robert Blair Wilkie and R. E. Muirhead, speakers at a public demonstration in Strathaven, 29th August 1952, in remembrance of Pearly Wilson, the local radical leader and martyr.

By courtesy the Radio Times

Drawing by Edward Gage, commissioned by the *Radio Times* to illustrate the advertised broadcast of *A Drunk Man Looks at the Thistle* by Hugh MacDiarmid.

Left to right—Matt Somerville, C.M.G., Oliver Brown, R. E. Muirhead, George Hamilton and Andrew Tannahill, members of the Scottish National Congress taking part in the May Day march organised by Glasgow Trades Council, Glasgow District Labour Party and the Co-operative Party, from George Square to Queen's Park in Glasgow in 1952. The Scottish National Congress was an umbrella group for all nationalist factions and they had their own speakers who addressed a crowd at the rally held in Queen's Park that day.

## THE PARROT CRY

Tell me the auld, auld story
O' hoo the Union brocht
Puir Scotland into being
As a country worth a thocht.
England, frae whom 'a blessings flow
What could we dae withoot ye?
Then dinna threip it doon oor throats
As gin we e'er could doot ye!
    My feelings lang wi' gratitude
    Ha'e been sae sairly harrowed
    That dod! I think it's time
    The claith was owre the parrot!

*Photos', William Kellock*

Ian Kellock with "Scotland Yet" placard, Ian Grant with "Scots Beef" placard. Middle row—Oliver Brown, Calum Campbell, C.M.G. Front row—Mrs Margaret Campbell, Matt Somerville, Wendy Wood and Valda Grieve.

*Photo: Gordon Wright*

Laurence Bradshaw, F.R.B.S., and C.M.G. first met in London in 1927 at the studio of the artist William McCance and his wife, the painter and wood engraver, Agnes Miller Parker.

Laurence Bradshaw sculpted two busts of C.M.G. in his studio in Warwick Road, London, in 1954. C.M.G. gave two sittings of thirty minutes each, from which the sculptures were completed.

The second version, showing C.M.G.'s hand, depicts the sculptor's impression of the poet reciting at the Institute of Contemporary Art, London, the same year. Both versions have been exhibited at different times at the Society of Portrait Sculptors in London. The first version has been exhibited in St James's Palace, London, Moscow, Prague and Bratislava. The second version was exhibited in St Paul's Cathedral, London, at an exhibition to mark Human Rights Year.

Laurence Bradshaw is also the author of the Karl Marx monument in Highgate Cemetery, London, and the Hannan Swaffer Memorial bust in the Press Club, Fleet Street, London.

*Photo: William Kellock*

Left to right—C.M.G., Wendy Wood and Hamish Henderson, photographed outside the High Kirk of St Giles, Edinburgh, in July 1954, after taking part in a cavalcade and demonstration of welcome for the release of four prisoners who had served part of a twelve-month prison sentence for conspiring to blow up St Andrew's House, the British Government's central office of administration in Edinburgh.

## O EASE MY SPIRIT

*"And as for their appearances, they four had one likeness, as if a wheel had been in the midst of a wheel."*

 EZEKIEL

O ease my spirit increasingly of the load
Of my personal limitations and the riddling differences
Between man and man with a more constant insight
Into the fundamental similarity of all activites.

And quicken me to the gloriously and terribly illuminating
Integration of the physical and the spiritual till I feel how easily
I could put my hand gently on the whole round world
As on my sweetheart's head and draw it to me.

95

Portrait photograph by Stephens Orr, 2nd December 1954.

*Photo: Scotland's Magazine*

Meeting at a favourite Edinburgh rendezvous, The Abbotsford, in Rose Street, Edinburgh, in 1955. Left to right—C.M.G., Valda Grieve, Donald Cameron, Callum Macdonald, printer and publisher of the Scottish literary magazine *Lines Review,* and Sydney Goodsir Smith. The first number of *Lines* was conceived by Alan Riddell and printed by Joseph Mardell of Serif Books. It was launched in 1952 in honour of Hugh MacDiarmid's sixtieth birthday. Callum Macdonald took over printing and publication from the second issue and C.M.G. became a member of the magazine's advisory board from issue number four until the resumed publication of his own *Voice of Scotland* Vol. V., No. 4, in January 1955.

Photo: The Glasgow Herald

Mrs Valda Grieve, C.M.G. and Roland E. Muirhead, "Father of the Scottish Nationalist Movement".

On Tuesday, 11th September 1956, in the McEwan Hall, Edinburgh, R. E. Muirhead was presented with the Andrew Fletcher of Saltoun Medal for "Service to Scotland" by Edinburgh University Nationalist Club.

In a published tribute to R. E. Muirhead, "The Significance of R. E. Muirhead", C.M.G. concluded with these words:

> "Mr Muirhead is now an octogenarian. It is unlikely that the cause to which he has devoted himself will now prevail in his lifetime. If that is so, still there can be little doubt that 'a dead man will win the fight'. It is this surety of ultimate victory that has sustained Mr Muirhead. Like Hardie he is not a 'mere politician'. If a Parliament re-established in Edinburgh has not yet been secured, a great deal has been accomplished for the reintegration of Scotland in the past thirty years, and Mr Muirhead's has been 'the yeast that has leavened the lump', a pervasive influence that has more or less unobtrusively nourished everything radically Scottish. In any other country in the world he would have been recognised as a Grand Old Man of his people. In Scotland if he has not been able to compete for the regard of his compatriots with royalties, film stars, golf champions, English carpet baggers and all the other riff-raff on whom the spotlight concentrates, I have no doubt that he will be fittingly recognised in time as a salutory force at the roots of our national existence, as one who in a time of sad distortion of all Scottish interests and values kept a way open for a return to our true tradition, and as a human being who in his gentleness and generosity and unselfishness sums up in his own character all those qualities which however they may be discounted by 'smart Alecs' are nevertheless essential to the ultimate achievement in our country of anything really worth while in any field of endeavour."

C.M.G. was first sculpted by Benno Schotz in 1941. The plaster bust was sent to London for the Society of Portrait Sculptors' exhibition, but due to the pressures of the war, the bust was never retrieved and afterwards lost.

In 1958 a television arts programme, "Counterpoint", jointly edited by George Bruce and Maurice Lindsay, was broadcast from the B.B.C. studios in Glasgow.

During the programme Maurice Lindsay interviewed Sir William O. Hutchison, P.R.S.A., Sir Alexander Gray, and Hugh MacDiarmid talked on "The deterioration of the Scottish face".

During the broadcast, Benno Schotz sculpted a bust of MacDiarmid in terra-cotta. There were two cameras prepared to cover the speakers and the sculptor, but prior to transmission, the camera which was to record the speakers failed and the eventual transmission mainly consisted of Benno Schotz sculpting.

The terra-cotta which was produced in twenty-three minutes of the programme was gifted by the sculptor to the B.B.C. and now stands in the boardroom of their headquarters in Glasgow.

C.M.G. and his wife spent the night with Mr and Mrs Schotz at their home in Glasgow and the following morning C.M.G. posed in the sculptor's studio and a new plaster bust was completed within three hours.

The first cast, purchased by the Scottish Arts Council, is on loan to The Saltire Society and on permanent display at their headquarters in Gladstone's Land, Edinburgh.

The second cast was purchased by the B.B.C. and is on display at their headquarters in Glasgow.

*Photos: Benno Schotz*

A party from the British-Chinese Friendship Society embarking for China at Heathrow Airport, London, in 1957. The company includes, fifth from left, C.M.G.; eighth, Beryl de Zoete; ninth and tenth, Countess and Earl of Huntingdon; eleventh, Basil Taylor of the Oriental Department of the British Museum. During this visit C.M.G. met Chairman Mao Tse Tung and Chun-Li.

C.M.G. at a reception in the People's Hall, Peking, talking to Kuo-mo-jo, the Chinese poet and cultural leader.

Speaking to a gathering in Peking to honour William Blake and Walt Whitman.

Photo: The Glasgow Herald

On 5th July 1957, C.M.G. received an honorary LL.D. from Edinburgh University. In the photograph he is being capped by Sir Edward Appleton, Principal of the University, at the ceremony in the McEwan Hall, Edinburgh.

Photo: Edinburgh Evening News

The group of honorary graduates. Front row, left to right—Dr Michael Ramsay, the Archbishop of York, the Countess of Rosebery, Sir Edward Appleton, Principal of the University, Sir Sydney Smith, Rector, Professor Max Born, Rev. John K. S. Reid. Back row, left to right—Sir Howard W. Florey, Sir John S. Macpherson, Rev. Henry C. Duncan, Lord Thomson, Sir John Storrar, Rev. R. Leonard Small and C.M.G. After the ceremony, Sir Sydney Smith gave a wine reception for the honorary graduates and in the evening Norman MacCaig held a party in his house for C.M.G. and friends.

Left to right—Alexander Scott, Alec McCrindle, C.M.G., Norman MacCaig, William Gallacher, Communist M.P. for West Fife, and Benno Schotz, R.S.A., photographed at a party organised by the Scottish Secretariat of the Communist Party of Great Britain to celebrate C.M.G.'s sixty-fifth birthday, Glasgow 1957.

*Photo: The Glasgow Herald*

Left to right—C.M.G., Robert Blair Wilkie, Mr Andrew Hood, Lord Provost of Glasgow, and Mrs Valda Grieve, at a dinner in the Grand Hotel, Glasgow, organised by the Scottish National Congress to honour C.M.G. who was presented with a pipe to commemorate the occasion, 17th January 1958.

*Photo: Edinburgh Evening News*

Left to right—Mr Alec Clark, President of the Edinburgh University Nationalist Club, C.M.G. and Mrs Valda Grieve, on the occasion of the presentation to C.M.G. of the Andrew Fletcher of Saltoun Medal for "Service to Scotland", at the University Theatre, Adam House, Edinburgh, 10th May 1958.

*Photo: Edinburgh Evening News*

Left to right—Gordon Wilson, secretary of the Edinburgh University Nationalist Club, C.M.G. and Helen B. Cruickshank, who presented C.M.G. with his portrait by Barbara Niven (1935) as part of the Andrew Fletcher Award.

103

*The Scottish Journal,* published by William MacLellan of Glasgow, ran for twelve issues from September 1952 until the issue dated January/April 1954. C.M.G. had poems, articles and reviews published, contributing to almost every issue.

ST ANDREWS UNIVERSITY RECTORIAL ELECTION, 1958

| | |
|---|---|
| Lord Boothby | 723 |
| Sir Charles MacAndrew | 520 |
| Sir John Glubb | 428 |
| Dr C. M. Grieve | 262 |

RECTOR—Lord Boothby

*Photo: Cyril Maitland*

C.M.G. in Milne's Bar,
"The Poets' Pub",
Hanover Street,
Edinburgh,
in the late
fifties.

35 HANOVER STREET  EDINBURGH 2  CALEDON'AN  6738

## MILNE'S BAR

### Luncheons and Snacks

### m e n u

| | |
|---|---|
| SOUP | |
| **ENTREES** | |
| Steak Mince, Beans or Peas & Potatoes | 8d. |
| Steak & Kidney Pie, Beans or Peas & Potatoes | 2/4 |
| ½ Steak & Kidney Pie, Stew, Beans or Peas & Potatoes | 2/1 |
| Stewed Steak, Beans or Peas & Potatoes | 2/1 |
| Braised Sausages, Beans or Peas & Potatoes | 2/4 |
| Mince Pie, Beans or Peas, & Potatoes | 1/9 |
| ½ Steak & Kidney Pie, Mince, Beans or Peas & Potatoes | 1/6 |
| 2 Mince Pies, Mince, Beans or Peas & Potatoes | 2/1 |
| Cold Gammon, Veg., Beans or Peas & Potatoes | 2/10 |
| Boiled Eggs | 3/- |
| Biscuits and Cheese | 7d. |
| Sandwiches, Various | 9d. |
| **COFFEE** | 9d. |
| White | Per Cup |
| Black | |
| **TEA** | 6d. |
| | 4d. |
| | 5d. |

*Photo: The Scotsman*

Sydney Goodsir Smith, C.M.G. and Norman
MacCaig, photographed at the first 200
Burns Club supper in the Peacock Hotel,
Newhaven, Edinburgh, 20th January 1959.

The
**200 BURNS CLUB**

Bards
HUGH MACDIARMID
NORMAN McCAIG
SYDNEY GOODSIR SMITH

President
Dr. DAVID ORR

Secretary
JAMES CRICHTON

Howff
MILNE'S BAR
Hanover Street
Edinburgh

MEMBERSHIP and SUBSCRIPTION
CARD

Photo: The Glasgow Herald

The 200 Burns Club supper at The Lea Rig Bar, Bo'ness, in 1960. Left to right—Willie Kellock, chairman of the Bo'ness Rebels Literary Society (who hosted this supper) and chairman for the evening, C.M.G. and Dr Tom Scott.

In 1958 Dr David Orr, James Crichton and C.M.G. met to discuss the formation of a Burns club which would celebrate the forthcoming bicentenary of the birth of Robert Burns and through its existence encourage new Scottish writing. The club was named the 200 Burns Club and the members met at Milne's Bar, Hanover Street, Edinburgh.

A special envelope, with a vignette of Burns by Aba Bayevsky, was printed and Dr Orr and James Crichton addressed invitations of membership to heads of state throughout the world. It was proposed to post these in Ayr on the anniversary day, 25th January 1959, and have them franked by the post office. To those who accepted, this would serve as proof of founder membership. But the unforeseen arose when the Postmaster in Ayr refused to frank an envelope which positioned a vignette in place of the monarch's head, so the special envelopes were despatched inside ordinary envelopes.

The club attracted many enthusiasts and replies with good wishes were received from the offices of General Eisenhower, Harold MacMillan and Jawaharlal Nehru.

The first 200 Burns Club supper was held in the Peacock Hotel, Newhaven, Edinburgh, on Friday, 20th January 1959, and C.M.G., Sydney Goodsir Smith and Norman MacCaig were installed as club bards.

Since its inception in 1959, the club has held many suppers and financed the publication of an edition of *A Drunk Man Looks at the Thistle* by Hugh MacDiarmid, and *Scottish Noel* by Fionn Mac Colla.

During a tour of
Czechoslovakia,
Rumania, Bulgaria
and Hungary on the
occasion of the Burns
bicentenary celebrations, 1959.
Seen here giving
the Burns oration
in Prague.

C.M.G. relaxing with
Mr Arnost Vanacek,
secretary of the writers'
union of Czechoslovakia
and an interpreter, 1959.

C.M.G. giving a Burns
bicentenary address
in Bucharest. The
platform party are all
well-known Rumanian
writers.

*Photo: The Alloa Journal*

C.M.G. and Mrs Henry Murray, wife of the proprietor and editor of the *Alloa Journal*. Taken at the Press Ball, the Golden Lion Hotel, Stirling, 1959.

*Photo: Daily Record*

Left to right—Caroline Rait, concert artiste, Thornton Wilder, the American novelist and playwright, and C.M.G. at a lunch party in the North British Hotel, Edinburgh, during the International Festival, 1959.

John Ogden, internationally famous pianist, and C.M.G. with Ronald Stevenson at his home in West Linton, Peeblesshire, 1st December 1959, when Ogden gave a private performance of *Opus Clavicembalisticum* by Kaikhosru Sorabji, which the composer dedicated to Hugh MacDiarmid.

*Photo: Helmut Petzsch*

# THE BATTLE OF TRIPE

**THAT other election was forgotten in the quadrangle of Aberdeen University's Marischal College yesterday.**

While President John Kennedy fought his way to the White House with words Aberdeen student supporters of birdman Peter Scott — for rector — fought theirs with TRIPE.

It was the traditional pre-election fight by rival factions who wanted to "let off steam" before Saturday's voting for the new rector.

No Democratic convention could have done better.

### Fish heads flay them

Armed with tripe, entrails, bags of soot and peasemeal, the army of Peter Scott moved into battle like a V-formation flight of his ducks.

And squawks came from their rival finalists, supporters of Scots poet Hugh MacDiarmid, as tripe, fish heads and what-have-you flayed them.

And there were a few intellectually muttered four-letter words as one enthusiastic Scott man tried to drag down the MacDiarmid shield, nailed high on a barricaded door.

### Rotten eggs

The MacDiarmid men went down fighting. They had two short, sharp successful encounters against supporters of speed ace Donald Campbell and shipping magnate Sir Colin Anderson.

They pelted rotten eggs, filled the air with clouds of sulphur and whiting "bombs". Rotten melons were tossed about like grenades.

And by the end of the day nobody recognised who was for whom in the fog of battle and bursting squibs.

*Scottish Daily Express* report.

ABERDEEN UNIVERSITY RECTORIAL ELECTION, 1960

| | |
|---|---|
| Peter Scott | 277 |
| C. M. Grieve | 248 |
| Cliff Michelmore | 188 |
| Sir Colin Anderson | 187 |
| Donald Campbell | 85 |

Rector—Peter Scott

Sydney Goodsir Smith, C.M.G. and Norman MacCaig caricatured in The Abbotsford pub, Rose Street, Edinburgh, by Moira Crichton, 1960.

EMPTY VESSEL

I met ayont the cairney
A lass wi' tousie hair
Singing' till 'a bairnie
That was nae langer there.

Wunds wi warlds to swing
Dinna sing sae sweet,
The licht that bends owre a'thing
Is less ta'en up wi't.

112

Photo: Associated Press Ltd.

C.M.G. addressing a huge rally in London's Trafalgar Square, 18th February 1961, at the start of a civil disobedience campaign against nuclear weapons launched by Earl Russell (Bertrand Russell, the philosopher). After the rally, Earl Russell and other members of the Committee of 100 led 2,200 volunteers down Whitehall to the Ministry of Defence to stage a three-hour sit-down protest.

Sir Herbert Read, formerly Professor of Fine Arts at Edinburgh University and author of many books on modern art and literary subjects, addressing the crowd. Seated on the platform— C.M.G., Lady Russell and Earl Bertrand Russell.

*Photo: Michael Peto*

Dr David Orr and C.M.G. leaving Brownsbank for a 200 Burns Club supper.

*Photo: The Associated Press*

C.M.G. is presented with the William Foyle Poetry Prize (£250) for 1962 by Mr William Foyle at a literary luncheon in his honour, at the Dorchester Hotel, Park Lane, London, 14th March 1963. The luncheon was attended by many friends and admirers including Mr Michael Noble, the Secretary of State for Scotland. During the proceedings, Dame Sybil Thorndike read one of C.M.G.'s poems. After the luncheon C.M.G. recorded a broadcast for the B.B.C.

## About that Terrible Infant, Hugh MacDiarmid

# THE GREAT LOVE AFFAIR

## A MAN AND HIS COUNTRY

On 11th August that famous Terrible Infant, Hugh MacDiarmid, will at last have grown up to the maturity of the allotted span. Another way of putting it is that on 11th August that distinguished Scottish Man of Letters, Christopher Murray Grieve, Doctor of Laws in the University of Edinburgh, will celebrate his 70th birthday " magna cum laude."

Whichever way you look at it, and it must be allowed that most people will look at it in the former way, this particular birthday will be celebrated with a certain and proper pomp.

In the first place, the Terrible Infant will be presented with his portrait, painted by R. H. Westwater, A.R.S.A., R.P., and subscribed for by his many friends and admirers in Scotland and abroad.

This portrait is eventually destined to hang alongside those of other famous Scots in the National Portrait Gallery in Edinburgh.

At the same time, Messrs Oliver & Boyd will publish the British edition of his " Collected Poems "; a new edition of the poet's masterpiece, " A Drunk Man Looks at the Thistle," will be published by the 200 Burns Club of Edinburgh, and K. D Duval will publish a book of essays, tributes and reminiscences on, to and about the Bard by many distinguished writers, entitled somewhat esoterically " Hugh MacDiarmid, A Festschrift."

THE PORTRAIT . . . it will hang beside other famous Scots in the National Portrait Gallery.

## by Sydney Goodsir Smith

Doubtless other things are planned to celebrate the occasion but these are the most important.

They are in sum and in particular an expression of the gratitude of many men and women for the services the Terrible Infant has rendered to Scottish life and thought over the last half century or so.

Hugh MacDiarmid has many friends; he also has many enemies. Like him or hate him, he is a phenomenon. You can ignore him no more than you can ignore the weather.

He has spent his life being à thorn in the flesh to all that is smug, complacent and ignorant in the life of modern Scotland—for her own good! Naturally, this has been resented. But it has had an effect for all that.

Resentment, however, has been powerless to touch him, for he has been living on disapproval, as other artists live on flattery, all his days.

Indeed, disapproval, for him, has been a kind of flattery. If love and hate are opposite sides of the same coin, then MacDiarmid has been carrying on a love affair with Scotland, and she with him, for 70 years.

Let us hope that at last she has opened her arms to him. It is not before time.

And when all the speeches are spoke and all the ink is dry, when all the plots have thickened and all the hatchets buried, what will eventually remain will be a body of poetry unmatched in Scotland since the great days of Burns and, indeed, unmatched in the world in the present century.

The Rose of all the World is not for me.
All I want for my part
Is the little white rose of Scotland
That smells sweet, and breaks the heart.

" He established himself as the new prophetic voice of Scotland. . . . Founder member of the Scottish National Party, off and on an active Communist, a militant anglophobe with a magnificent English style . . . his life was dedicated to the regeneration of the Scottish literary language."
—From Chambers's Biographical Dictionary.

COIA

116

*Photo: Gordon Wright*

Pen and ink portrait by commercial artist Moira Crichton, 1962.

## SCOTLAND SMALL?

Scotland small? Our multiform, our infinite Scotland *small?*
Only as a patch of hillside may be a cliché corner
To a fool who cries "Nothing but heather!" Where in September another
Sitting there and resting and gazing round
Sees not only heather but blaeberries
With bright green leaves and leaves already turned scarlet,
Hiding ripe blue berries; and amongst the sage-green leaves
Of the bog-myrtle the golden flowers of the tormentil shining;
And on the small bare places, where the little Blackface sheep
Found grazing, milkworts blue as summer skies;
And down in neglected peat-hags, not worked
In living memory, sphagnum moss in pastel shades
Of yellow, green, and pink; sundew and butterwort
And nodding harebells vying in their colour
With the blue butterflies that poise themselves delicately upon them.
And stunted rowans with harsh dry leaves of glorious colour
"Nothing but heather!" — How marvellously descriptive! And incomplete!

117

*Photo: John Dewar*

Photograph of C.M.G. and publisher Kulgin Duval taken at a party in Gladstone's Land, Lawnmarket, Edinburgh, to mark the publication of *MacDiarmid: a Festschrift,* composed for C.M.G.'s seventieth birthday. About one hundred guests from the arts and literary world attended the party.

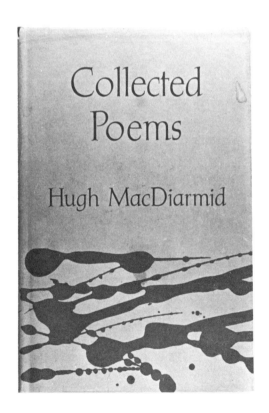

The first edition of the *Collected Poems* of Hugh MacDiarmid was published by the MacMillan Company, New York, in 1962. Mr Robin Lorimer, then general editor of Oliver and Boyd, the Edinburgh publishers, was able to persuade his directors to purchase one thousand sets of sheets from MacMillan for publication in the U.K. under their own imprint.

The one thousand copies, published in late August 1962, sold out in three weeks.

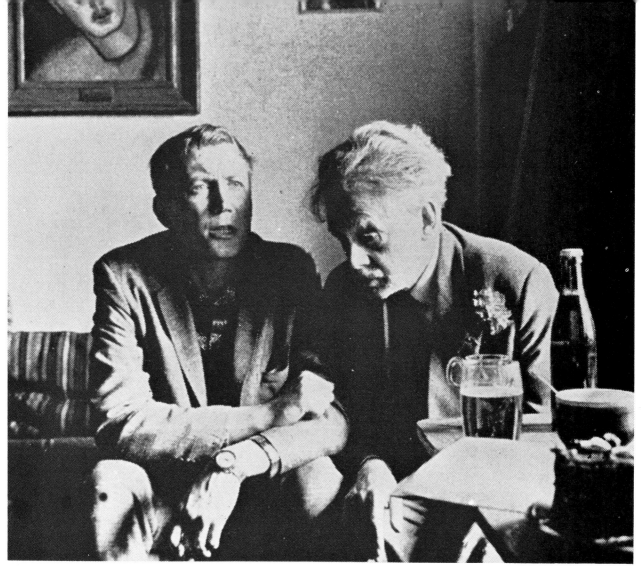

*Photo: Michael Peto*

An early morning visit from Russian Poet Yevgeny Yevtushenko to C.M.G. at his home, Brownsbank, in May 1962.

24 York Place,
Edinburgh 1.

This year sees Hugh MacDiarmid's seventieth birthday. By way of marking the occasion we are proposing to present him with his portrait, which will subsequently go to the Scottish National Portrait Gallery.

In view of his distinguished services to Scottish literature, we are sure that many Scots and admirers of his work will wish to be associated with this project.

Subscriptions, which will be acknowledged, should be sent to Hugh MacDiarmid Presentation Fund, Clydesdale and North of Scotland Bank, Dalmeny Street Branch, 295 Leith Walk, Edinburgh 6.

> Appleton, John Bannerman, Boothby, Helen
> Cruickshank, David Daiches, Neil M. Gunn,
> Norman MacCaig, Compton Mackenzie, Albert
> Mackie, William MacTaggart, Naomi Mitchison,
> Abe Moffat, Sydney Goodsir Smith, John Tainsh.

*Scottish Field*, 1962.

*Photo: The Glasgow Herald*

Left to right—Benno Schotz, R. H. Westwater, A.R.S.A., R.P., the artist, and C.M.G. Benno Schotz presented C.M.G. with his portrait by R. H. Westwater which was commissioned by his friends to honour him on his seventieth birthday. Edinburgh, 22nd August 1962.

*Photo: Tom Scott*

Left to right—Ronald Stevenson, Dmitri Schostakovich and C.M.G. at a presentation ceremony in the George Hotel, Edinburgh, during the International Festival of 1962.

Between 1960 and 1962, Ronald Stevenson composed his Passacaglia on DSCH for piano. It is based on the initials of its dedicatee, Dmitri Schostakovich — DSCH in German nomenclature, that is D, E flat, C, B.

C.M.G. presided over the ceremony when Ronald Stevenson presented Schostakovich with a complete copy of the work.

The above photograph is an enlarged frame of a 16-millimetre ciné film. The only photographic record of the occasion which captured the three together.

LOVE

A luvin' wumman is a licht
That shows a man his waefu' plight,
Bleezin' steady on ilka bane,
Wrigglin' sinnen an' twinin' vein,
Or fleerin' quick an' gane again,
An' the mair scunnersome the sicht
The mair for luve an' licht he's fain
Till clear an' chitterin' an' nesh
Move a' the miseries o' his flesh.

121

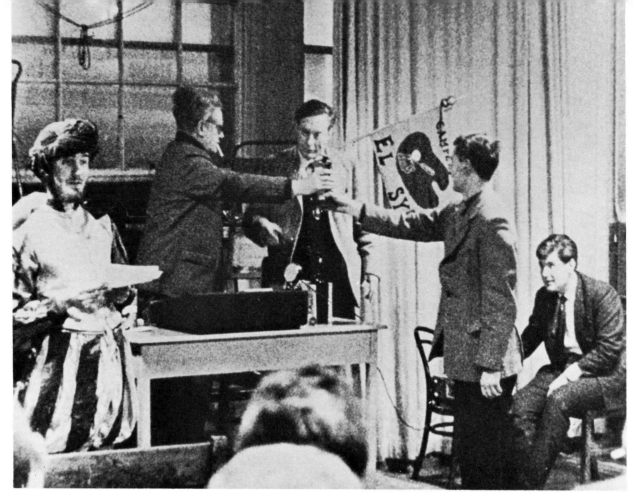

*Photo: Alan Daiches*

Central figures left to right—C.M.G., Sydney Goodsir Smith and Iain Holroyd. C.M.G., president, presents Sydney Goodsir Smith with the Sir Thomas Urquhart Award (an engraved tankard) on behalf of the Edinburgh University Scottish Renaissance Society for his services to Scottish literature. The S.R.C. Hall, Old College, Edinburgh, 14th December 1962.

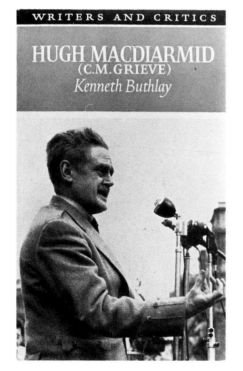

Kenneth Buthlay's *Hugh MacDiarmid* in the Oliver and Boyd, Writers and Critics series, 1964.

*Photos: Gordon Wright*

Left to right, front row — C.M.G., William Gallacher, M.P., Phil Paraten and Abe Moffat, a Scottish miners' leader. At a party in Glasgow held by the Communist Party for C.M.G.'s seventieth birthday, 1963.

## FOCHERTY

Duncan Gibb o' Focherty's
A giant to the likes o' me,
His face is like a roarin' fire
For love o' the barley-bree.

He gangs through this and the neebrin' shire
Like a muckle rootless tree
—And here's a caber for Daith to toss
That'll gi'e his spauld a swee!

His gain was aye a wee'r man's loss
And he took my lass frae me,
An wi' mony a quean besides
He's ta'en his liberty.

I've had nae chance wi' the likes o' him
And he's tramped me underfit
—Blaefaced afore the throne o' God
He'll get his fairin' yet.

He'll be like a bull in the sale-ring there,
And I'll lauch lood to see,
Till he looks up and canna mak' oot
Whether it's God—or me!

# HUGH MacDIARMID CHOSEN TO OPPOSE PREMIER

## FROM A POLITICAL CORRESPONDENT

WESMINSTER, Thursday.

The Communist Party today announced the selection of Dr C. M. Grieve (Hugh MacDiarmid, the poet) as their prospective candidate for Kinross and West Perthshire in the General Election. The party have chosen the Premier's constituency as the arena for a challenge on the election broadcasting arrangements between the major political parties.

At a news conference at the Communist Party Headquarters in King Street, Covent Garden, London, this afternoon, Dr Grieve made it clear that his candidature was a challenge on the broadcasting issue.

If, during the course of the General Election campaign, Sir Alec Douglas-Home appears in any political broadcast, Dr Grieve will request similar facilities from the broadcasting authorities. If his request is refused, he will seek to get the election in West Perthshire annulled on the grounds of a breach of election law.

Dr Grieve argued that whether Sir Alec speaks over radio or television as Prime Minister or as Conservative candidate for West Perthshire and Kinross, he will still be seeking personal votes in his constituency, and that the other candidates should be entitled to similar facilities.

Asked whether his candidature would not split the Scottish nationalist vote in the constituency, in view of his well-known support of the Scottish nationalist cause, Dr Grieve said that he had known Mr Arthur Donaldson, the chairman of the Scottish National Party and candidate in West Perthshire, for 40 years. They had discussed the matter and Mr Donaldson agreed that there would not be a split in Scottish national support.

Of his opponent, Sir Alec Douglas-Home, Dr Grieve said: "He is in fact a zombie, personifying the obsolescent traditions of an aristocratic and big landlord order, of which Thomas Carlyle said that no country had been oppressed by a worse gang of hyenas than Scotland.

"He is not really a Scotsman, of course, but only a sixteenth part of one, and all his education and social affiliations are anti-Scottish.

"Sir Walter Scott warned long ago that a Scotsman unscotched would become only a damned mischievous Englishman, and that is precisely what has happened in this case."

*The Scotsman* report, 4th September 1964.

Photo: *The Scotsman*

Alex Clark, Election Agent, C.M.G. and John Gollan, former General Secretary of the Communist Party of Great Britain.

*Daily Record*

"A is for Arms Bill, paid out of tax, B is for Beeching, the man with the axe . . . it doesn't sound like Hugh MacDiarmid's kind of stuff to me!"

*The Scotsman*, Monday, 21st September 1964. Coia's view of Kinross and West Perthshire.

GENERAL ELECTION, 15th October 1964 (Kinross and West Perthshire)

| | |
|---|---|
| Sir Alec Douglas-Home (Con.) | 16,659 |
| A. Forrester (Lab.) | 4,687 |
| A. Donaldson (Scot. Nat.) | 3,522 |
| Dr C. M. Grieve (Comm.) | 127 |

# DR GRIEVE TO GET HIS £1,000 BACK

Dr Christopher Grieve (Hugh MacDiarmid, the poet), who was ordered to pay the expenses in his unsuccessful petition to unseat Sir Alec Douglas-Home after last year's General Election, was given permission yesterday to recover the £1,000 he lodged as security. Lord Migdale was told in the Election Court that Dr Grieve had now settled the expenses of the action.

Dr Grieve lodged the money on deposit receipt under the Representation of the People Act 1949, within three days of presenting his petition. The Election Court in December declared Sir Alec "duly elected" as M.P. for Kinross and West Perthshire and held that no corrupt or illegal practice had been proved to have been committed.

Dr Grieve had contended that expenditure on party political broadcasts were not included in Sir Alec's return of election expenses, and asked the court to declare the election void. Lord Migdale, who presided, was satisfied that neither Sir Alec, the B.B.C. nor I.T.A. had been in breach of the Act. Lord Kilbrandon agreed and the court awarded expenses against Dr Grieve.

### EXPENSES SETTLED

In court yesterday, Mr D. B. Smith, advocate for Dr Grieve, told Lord Migdale that the expenses had now been settled and he moved that the deposit be returned.

The judge commented that the expenses did not come up to the amount of the deposit and as Dr Grieve had paid all expenses, he was now entitled to recover the deposit. He directed that the accountant of court should hand over the deposit receipt.

Judge—Lord Migdale.

Counsel for Dr Grieve—Mr D. B. Smith. Solicitors-Drummond & Reid, S.S.C., Edinburgh.

*The Scotsman* report, 21st July 1965.

Left to right—Major Hume Sleigh, Moray MacLaren and C.M.G. on the occasion of the presentation to Major Sleigh of his portrait in the Paperback Bookshop, Edinburgh. Major Sleigh was a member of the Scottish Patriots and a lifelong activist for Scotland's independence.

Line drawing of C.M.G. by Leonard Penrice, July 1966. This was one of six drawings commissioned for the publication *Poems to Hugh MacDiarmid on his Seventy-fifth Birthday*, Duncan Glen, 1967.

Photo: courtesy Duncan Glen

C.M.G.'s relationship with Duncan Glen began in 1962 when Glen wrote to him to check several points for the book he had written, *Hugh MacDiarmid and the Scottish Renaissance*.

Duncan Glen had discovered the poetry of Hugh MacDiarmid in the early nineteen-fifties and by the early sixties, as a professional typographic designer with a passionate enthusiasm for MacDiarmid's work, his thoughts turned to the possibility of producing fine printings of his poems. However, Duncan Glen's first publication was his own essay, *Hugh MacDiarmid: Rebel Poet and Prophet*, published as a tribute to both aspects of MacDiarmid's character on his seventieth birthday, 11th August 1962, shortly after their first meeting at Brownsbank in July of that year. This was a short edition of fifty-five copies published under his imprint, The Drumalban Press, and priced at 10/6. Each copy was signed by Duncan Glen.

Glen's second publication, MacDiarmid's poem, *Poetry like the Hawthorn*, was handset and printed by Glen in a limited edition of one hundred and twenty-five copies at 3/6 and twenty-five copies signed by MacDiarmid at 10/6. When this was published in September 1962, C.M.G. wrote to Glen, "An elegant job, beautifully printed and produced."

Since 1962 Duncan Glen has published, through his magazine *Akros* or by individual title, thirty-seven articles of poetry and prose by MacDiarmid or relating to MacDiarmid and his work. An achievement and contribution to Scottish literature unequalled by any other publisher. Undoubtedly Glen's most important publication remains his own *Hugh MacDiarmid and the Scottish Renaissance* (Chambers, 1964), which gives a detailed study of MacDiarmid and his work and clearly establishes MacDiarmid's leadership in the Scottish Literary Renaissance of the twenties.

The Press welcomed the book as balanced, clear and immensely thorough. Duncan Glen has also edited *Selected Essays of Hugh MacDiarmid* (Cape, 1969) and *Hugh MacDiarmid, A Critical Survey* (Scottish Academic Press, 1971).

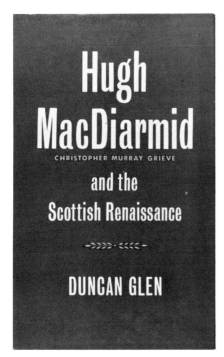  

*Photos: Gordon Wright*

Portrait of C.M.G. by William Johnstone drawn for the frontispiece of
*Hugh MacDiarmid and the Scottish Renaissance*, 1964.

I

C.M.G. and some of his lady friends at a reception in Glasgow in the sixties.

## LO! A CHILD IS BORN

I thought of a house where the stones seemed suddenly changed
And became instinct with hope, hope as solid as themselves,
And the atmosphere warm with that lovely heat,
The warmth of tenderness and longing souls, the smiling anxiety
That rules a home where a child is about to be born.
The walls were full of ears. All voices were lowered.
Only the mother had the right to groan or complain.
Then I thought of the whole world. Who cares for its travail
And seeks to encompass it in like loving kindness and peace?
There is a monstrous din of the sterile who contribute nothing
To the great end in view, and the future fumbles,
A bad birth, not like the child in that gracious home
Heard in the quietness turning in its mother's womb,
A strategic mind already, seeking the best way
To present himself to life, and at last, resolved,
Springing into history quivering like a fish,
Dropping into the world like a ripe fruit in due time—
But where is the Past to which Time, smiling through her tears
At her new-born son, can turn crying: "I love you"?

C.M.G. with two other lady friends.

MACDIARMID'S LYRICS

The tide goes over.
Not on my knees
These poems lie,
But the floor of existence.

Whelk and razorshell,
Delicate weight-lifters,
Supporting and made by
The crush of fathoms.

Norman MacCaig

*Photo: Gordon Wright*

C.M.G. sat for this portrait
by Aba Bayevsky in the
artist's studio during a visit
to Toronto in 1964.
The portrait was later purchased
by the 200 Burns Club
and presented to C.M.G. at
their annual Burns supper
on 28th January 1966 at
Bothkennar, Airth.

Portrait by
John Brown, 1968.

*Photo: Tom Scott*

*Photo: J. K. Annand*

Left to right—C.M.G., Helen B. Cruickshank and Ian Munro at H.B.C.'s eightieth birthday party at Ashgrove House the home of Joan and Fred Hunter, near Edinburgh. 15th May 1966.

*Photo: Oxford University Press*

Left to right—John MacQueen, William Montgomerie, Tom Scott, Helen B. Cruickshank, Joe Corrie, C.M.G., Douglas Young and Robert Garioch at a reception in Edinburgh given by the Clarendon Press on publication of the *Oxford Book of Scottish Verse* (edited by John MacQueen and Tom Scott) in 1966.

Photo: Gordon Wright

C.M.G., Oliver Brown and Dr Ian Taylor at the Press conference to launch the 1320 Club and the magazine *Catalyst*, December 1967.

The 1320 Club was formally set up in June 1967 by Dr Ian Taylor, Major F. A. C. Boothby, Russell Thomson and Edwin White, not as a political party, but with the political aim to prepare for the re-establishment of Scotland's sovereign independence by initiating various aspects of research.

Lord Boyd Orr accepted the patronage of the club and C.M.G. was appointed first president.

At a Press conference in Lucky MacLeuchar's Houff, 22 Minto Street, Edinburgh, in December 1967, the club was officially launched and the first issue of the club's magazine, *Catalyst*, was distributed to the members of the Press.

The first main event organised by Dr George Philp on behalf of the club was a symposium at Glasgow University on 6th April 1968. C.M.G. spoke on the motion "This house is in favour of self-government for Scotland" and a transcription of his speech was later published by Reprographia of Edinburgh as *A Political Speech*.

> *"These denationalised Scots have killed the soul*
> *Which is universally human; they are men without souls;*
> *All the more heavily the judgment falls upon them,*
> *Since it is a universal law of life they have sinned against."*

"There surely is the answer to the particular kind of treachery found in those Anglo-Scots intellectuals who bleat of a false antithesis, internationalism, not nationalism, as if it were possible to have the one without the other. They sin against the universal law of life which invests life in individuals not conglomerations. Yes, even in the ant hill. In the place of living separate identities, having mostly their differences in common, these ghouls would reduce all to a horrible international, characterless, abstract fog, a devitalised nonentity, but their internationalism in fact equals 'English', and behind the pseudo-internationalism of the Anglo-Scots lurks the face of 'The Auld Enemy', English imperialism."

On the death of Lord Boyd Orr in 1971, C.M.G. became Patron of the 1320 Club.

*Photos: Gordon Wright*

The main speakers at the 1320 Club symposium, 6th April 1968. Left to right—Dr George Davie, Nicholas Fairbairn, Q.C., C.M.G., Dr Gavin MacCrone and Professor Harry J. Hanham.

# 75th birthday exhibition for Hugh MacDiarmid

## By SYDNEY GOODSIR SMITH

To honour Christopher Murray Grieve ("Hugh MacDiarmid") on the occasion of his 75th Birthday, the National Library, George IV Bridge, Edinburgh, have put on a grand exhibition of the poet's first editions, manuscripts, letters, photographs, portrait drawing and paintings and a considerable number of rare, ephemeral publications in pamphlet or leaflet form — even the Broughton School magazine, where his first verses appeared.

The exhibition is very well mounted and the catalogue will become an important work of reference to future students.

Some of the portraits and caricatures are of great and curious interest, particularly his most recent portrait, painted by Rosalie Loveday, very characteristic, and a nice bit of painting, too, and the historic photograph of the Duke of Montrose, Cunninghame Graham, Compton Mackenzie, John MacCormick and the poet, taken on the occasion of the founding of the National Party of Scotland in the 1920s.

Mr M. A. Begg, who is responsible for the exhibition, and compiler of the catalogue, tells me that the collection is not absolutely complete — some items have vanished from human ken or been unavailable — but as it stands, covering every aspect of MacDiarmid's manifold activities as poet, journalist, propagandist and political candidate, it is a worthy tribute from Scotland's national library to Scotland's greatest modern poet.

The exhibition is open from 9.30 a.m. to 6 p.m., Monday to Friday, 9.30 a.m. to 1 p.m. on Saturdays, and 2 p.m. to 5 p.m. on Sundays. During the Festival it will remain open till 8.30 at night, Monday to Saturday.

*The Scotsman* report, 17th July 1967.

MacDiarmid

*Photo: Gordon Wright*

C.M.G. and Ronald Stevenson at Brownsbank.

Ronald Stevenson, the Scottish composer/pianist, has set more of Hugh MacDiarmid's poetry to music than any composer since F. G. Scott.

Stevenson's first MacDiarmid setting was "A'e Gowden Lyric", composed in the mid-sixties. Unlike Scott, his settings consist mainly of the later MacDiarmid poems and some of the prose.

Although he has written several short, separate song settings of MacDiarmid, Stevenson has also written two extended song cycles, "Border Boyhood", commissioned by Peter Pears, who premièred it with the composer at the 1971 Aldeburgh Festival; and "The Infernal City" (a song cycle about Glasgow and Edinburgh), commissioned by Duncan Robertson, who premiered it with the composer in London the same year.

In 1967 the B.B.C. commissioned Stevenson to compose a piano piece in honour of MacDiarmid's seventy-fifth birthday: the work that resulted was "Heroic Song for Hugh MacDiarmid". The composer has also published articles on MacDiarmid's work in relation to music.

137

Canvas with several studies of C.M.G. by Rosalie Loveday, 1967.

*Photos: Gordon Wright*

Miniature portrait by Rosalie Loveday, 1967.

Separatism.

If there's a sword-like sang
That can cut Scotland clear
O'a' the warld beside
Rax me the hilt o't here,

For there's nae jewel till
Frae the rest o' earth it's free,
Wi' the starry separateness
I'd fain to Scotland gi'e.

— Hugh MacDiarmid.

Portrait and poem print by Rosalie Loveday, 1968.

Seventy-sixth birthday portrait by Gordon Wright, 11th August 1968. In the same year, C.M.G. was elected an Honorary Fellow of the Modern Language Association of America.

*Photo: Gordon Wright*

Seventy-sixth birthday picture with Valda and F. Marian McNeill, 11th August 1968.

The LP record of Hugh MacDiarmid reading his own poetry was recorded in November 1968 and released by Claddagh Records Ltd., Dublin.

## The Bonnie Broukit Bairn

Mars is braw in crammasy,
Venus in a green silk goun,
The auld mune shak's her gowden feathers,
Their starry talk's a wheen o'blethers,
Nane for thee a thochtie sparin',
Earth, thou bonnie broukit bairn !
*—But greet, an' in your tears ye'll droun*
*The haill clanjamfrie !*

## HUGH MacDIARMID

Graphics by Birtley Aris      MidNAG Poetry Poster no. 21

Poetry poster published by Mid Northumberland Arts Group.

142

*Photo: Brian Evans*

Left to right—Mrs Irmi Mardersteig, Colin H. Hamilton, Mrs Valda Grieve, Dr Giovanni Mardersteig, C.M.G., Kulgin Duval and Mr and Mrs David Wright. Photograph taken in Langholm in 1970.

Dr Mardersteig founded the Officina Bodini in 1922 and it was transferred to Verona in 1927. Devoted to the production of hand-printed books, often illustrated by living artists, the books from the press are distinguished by the craftsmanship in the printing, and the design and production of the type face, many of which are designed by Dr Mardersteig himself.

Dr Mardersteig is widely regarded as the finest living printer and it is fortunate that two of Hugh MacDiarmid's books have been printed by him. *The Kind of Poetry I Want*, K. D. Duval, Edinburgh 1961, in an edition of 300 copies, and *A Drunk Man Looks at the Thistle*, Kulgin Duval and Colin H. Hamilton, Falkland 1969, in an edition of 160 copies, for which eight woodcuts were made by Frans Masereel who was specially commissioned by the publishers as his artistry contained much in common with that of the poet although working in different traditions.

The first complete edition of *Dìreadh I, II, III*, Kulgin Duval and Colin H. Hamilton, Frenich, Foss, 1974, in an edition of 200 copies, was printed by Dr Mardersteig's son, Martino, at the Stemperia Valdonega, an automated printing press which achieves an extremely high standard of commercial printing.

Collage portrait
by Jean White, 1970.

*Photos: Gordon Wright*

In 1972, Wm. Grant and Sons Ltd., the Scotch whisky distillers, created the honorary position of Governor of the Academy of Pure Malt Scotch Whisky to create knowledge and understanding of pure malt Scotch whisky. C.M.G. was one of seven distinguished men in the U.K. invited to become a Governor of the Academy.

For Hugh MacDiarmid

You've walked on the waters quieter than God,
just listening
for Leviathan whudding his tail,
or the infinitesimal sound
of plancton,
like midges hung in still air.

When I put my ear to the great conch of your words
they bawl and hiss
of a universe in labour;
and hush to a woman's sigh
and quiet
when her waters break for a birth.

Light glowers off the darkness of your sea,
breaks up in
a lowe o' fun, and gathers
again, endlessly reforming
over amoebic depths
where life's too wee for hearing—

over slums where your moving surface refracts a heaven
of stony stars,
or admits a glimmer
of sun; in its swell
draws up a million
delicate lives and deaths.

You never whored the moon, naming her seas
Tranquillity—
but in the neap of our times gave
bloodstream, clenched brain,
your own miraculous tide
to her reflective light.

Morven Cameron

Photo: *Gordon Wright*

145

K

C.M.G. with Helena Weigel, Bertolt Brecht's widow, who is now in charge of the Berliner Ensemble. Photo taken in East Germany in the late nineteen-sixties.

On Friday, 2nd June 1971, Claddagh Records of Dublin released a double LP recording of Hugh MacDiarmid reading his long poem sequence *A Drunk Man Looks at the Thistle*. To mark the occasion, the Scottish Arts Council gave a reception at their headquarters in Edinburgh.

*Photos: Valda Grieve*

C.M.G. and Ezra Pound in Venice, 1971.

C.M.G. and Ezra Pound started corresponding in the 1930s when they were both contributing to *The New Age* magazine. They had many friends in common, especially in connection with Major Douglas's Social Credit proposals. Photographed above during a visit to Verona in the autumn of 1971 to meet Dr Mardersteig the printer and Frans Masereel the artist, C.M.G., his wife, Kulgin Duval and Colin Hamilton drove to Venice to meet Ezra Pound at his home. Ezra Pound and Olga Rudge entertained the party to lunch at a restaurant adjacent to their home and then they walked together in St Mark's Square. Later they had coffee together in Florians famous restaurant before returning to Verona in the evening.

Photo: *The Glasgow Herald*

Arriving for the celebrations in Edinburgh are, left to right, Norman MacCaig, Sydney Goodsir Smith, C.M.G., Sorley MacLean and Professor Alastair Fowler. Friday, 27th May 1972.

To mark the forthcoming eightieth birthday of Dr C. M. Grieve (Hugh MacDiarmid), which falls in August, a gathering of academics and others spent yesterday at Edinburgh University discussing his poetry and its place in Scottish life and letters.

The principal event of the day was a public lecture by Professor David Daiches, of Sussex University, on "Hugh MacDiarmid and the Scottish Literary Traditions".

This was preceded by a "symposium" in the morning and afternoon, to which the chief contributors were Roderick Watson of Stirling University, and Edwin Morgan and Alexander Scott, of Glasgow University.

Some 45 persons took part in the symposium, representing six Scottish and two English universities, the Scottish Education Department, the British Council, the English Association, the National Library of Scotland, and other bodies and, together with others present in a private capacity, speaking for a wide range of interests in Scottish intellectual life.

*The Scotsman* report, 28th May 1972.

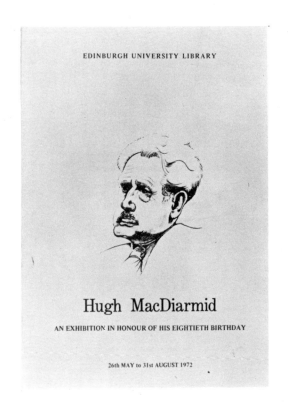

EDINBURGH UNIVERSITY LIBRARY

# Hugh MacDiarmid

AN EXHIBITION IN HONOUR OF HIS EIGHTIETH BIRTHDAY

26th MAY to 31st AUGUST 1972

By arrangement with Bernard Delfont

Michael White

presents

Vanessa Redgrave  Joe Melia
Ronald Radd  Annie Ross  Barbara Windsor
And Hermione Baddeley
in

# THE THREEPENNY OPERA

by Bertholt Brecht  music  Kurt Weill
English adaptation  Hugh MacDiarmid

with  Lon Satton.

Victor Maddern  Dan Meaden  Arthur Mullard
Derry Power   Henry Woolf

directed by  Tony Richardson
associate director  Keith Hack

sets by Patrick Robertson  costumes by Rosemary Vercoe
Lighting by Richard Pilbrow  Musical director Marcus Dods
Choreography Eleanor Fazan

Reduced Price Previews
Feb. 7 8 & 9 at 8·0  FIRST NIGHT FEB. 10 at 7·0
Subs. evgs. 8·0 Sats 6·0 & 8·40 Mat. Weds at 3·0

# PRINCE OF WALES THEATRE

Coventry Street  W1.  930·8681

The first performance of a new translation of *The Threepenny Opera* by Bertolt Brecht
and Kurt Weill, conflated by Hugh MacDiarmid from various other translations and
approved by the Brecht trustees, was given at the Prince of Wales Theatre, London, on
10th April 1972. It has since been performed by the English Music Theatre Company Ltd.
at Sadlers Wells, and is now included in their touring repertoire.

*Photo: Gordon Wright*

The bust of C.M.G. by Gillian Macdonald completed in 1972 when the sculptress was nineteen years old. The bust was later purchased by Glasgow University.

# To Hugh MacDiarmid, on his 80th birthday

## HAUD FORRIT

Over the years you've dreamed your dreams
And as always
You go back to your past
In Langholm—your tap-root.
Sometimes the past flows beside you
Like the Esk when partly hidden in the mist
Then there are these meetings in dreams—
Strange how sad they can be
Like Heine's grey ghost
That walked beside him
As he talked
Then again it's like a journey
In the sun and you look back
Over eighty years
Rather like looking back
After a long day's walk
Over Tarras Moor
And always in the background
The rivers Ewes and Wauchope
The sound of the Esk in high spate
Rising high and spilling over
Like you, MacDiarmid, ginny-truckled
Now you're awake
And find you're not an astronaut
Just a poet
Thousands of people and switches
Put Neil Armstrong on the Moon
You gripped the curly snake Cencrastus
And made it alone
Scars there will be in plenty
Let's hope they'll be in their natural creases
For your home-town is silent and indifferent *moonstruck*
Reaching out you find no welcoming hand
Hell! What need have you to care
You are meeting your eightieth year
Head held high, haud forrit MacDiarmid
Like Muhammad Ali—you're the greatest.

**Valda Trevlyn**
(Mrs Hugh MacDiarmid)

From *The Scotsman*, 12th August 1972.

The commemorative vignette issued by the Scottish Philatelic Secretariat to mark Hugh MacDiarmid's eightieth birthday. The vignette depicts a detail from the portrait of MacDiarmid by Aba Bayevsky.

# Moladh Mhic Dhiarmaid

(In praise of MacDiarmid)  IN HONOUR OF HIS EIGHTIETH BIRTHDAY  Piobaireachd by Alistair Keith Campsie

**URLAR**

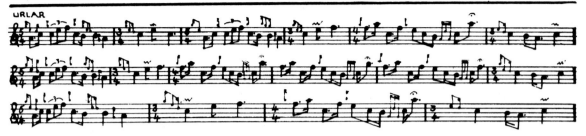

**FIRST VARIATION**

**SECOND VARIATION**

**TAORLUATH**

**CRUNLUATH**

**ABBREVIATIONS**

WRITTEN

PLAYED

On 15th December 1972 a small band of friends and admirers in Langholm presented C.M.G. with a leather chair as a belated eightieth birthday present. A group of mill workers raised £140 for the presentation which was made at a local hotel.

*Photo: Norman Allan*

*Photo: Gordon Wright*

In 1972, Mr Dave Harding, town artist of Glenrothes in Fife, produced three concrete cast paving stones of poems by Scottish poets in an attempt to incorporate literature into the external environment. Illustrated here is the cast of MacDiarmid's *The Little White Rose,* which is situated in the town centre.

153

John Montague, the Irish poet, and C.M.G. in Dublin 1973.

C.M.G. and Paddy Maloney, leader of The Chieftains, the Irish traditional instrumental group, Dublin, 1973.

*Photos: Irish Times*

Photo: courtesy Alan Thornhill

Bronze bust by Alan Thornhill, produced in a one-day sitting at Brownsbank, 8th December 1973. To be limited to six casts. This cast is in the possession of the sculptor.

Eighty-third birthday portrait by Gordon Wright.

*Photo: Gordon Wright*

Left to right—Sydney Goodsir Smith, J. B. Caird, George Davie, Sorley MacLean, C.M.G., Norman MacCaig and Iain Crichton Smith, photographed in the Scottish Arts Club, Edinburgh, after a dinner in Sorley MacLean's honour on his retiral from the headmastership of Plockton School and accepting the post of Writer in Residence to the University of Edinburgh, 16th February 1973.

C.M.G., Valda Grieve and Allen Ginsberg, at the Rotterdam International Poetry Festival, June 1973.

Photo: Gordon Wright

The Royal Scottish Academy, Edinburgh.

On 20th March 1974 C.M.G. was elected an honorary member of the Royal Scottish Academy of Painting, Sculpture and Architecture as the eighth Professor of Literature in consideration of his eminent talents as a poet and author and his services to the arts.

Photos: Valda Grieve

C.M.G. and his son Walter, 1975.     C.M.G. and his daughter Christine, 1975

Photo: Gordon Wright

C.M.G.'s eighty-third birthday with Valda, Michael, Deirdre and family, at Brownsbank, 11th August 1975.

Cartoon by "Tash" exhibited
at the Henderson Gallery
during the Edinburgh Festival
1975.

Brownsbank — C.M.G.'s house in the Lanarkshire hills, 1975.

## Hugh MacDiarmid records poems for 'phone-in'

Hugh MacDiarmid (81), a founder of the Scottish National Party, spent part of yesterday recording several of his poems in London for the Greater London Arts Council to be heard on the London telephone system.

After an evening paper published the dial-a-poem number — 836 3872 — the service last night became virtually unobtainable with queues of callers wanting to hear MacDiarmid.

Other poets who have similarly recorded their works are Cecil Day Lewis, Kingsley Amis and Spike Milligan.

The *Scotsman* report,
26th November 1973

## Film tribute to Scots poet

A short film commissioned by the Scottish Arts Council, and to be given its first showing during the Edinburgh Festival next month, will be part of the celebrations of Hugh MacDiarmid's eightieth birthday on August 11.

The film, "Hugh MacDiarmid: No Fellow Travellers", has been made by Ogam Films in association with the Films of Scotland Committee. It will be shown at a special poetry reading in Edinburgh on September 5, and is also to have television performances.

This is the second in the Scottish Arts Council's series of films about Scottish writers, the first, devoted to Neil Gunn, having been made last year. They are intended not only as personal tributes and permanent records, but also for classroom use in the teaching of Scottish literature.

*Glasgow Herald* report,
3rd August 1972

Photos: Gordon Wright

Left to right—Mrs Deirdre Grieve,
Miss Jean White, Mrs Valda Grieve,
C.M.G., Provost Gordon Murray and
Mr Michael Grieve on the occasion of
C.M.G. receiving the freedom of the
Burgh of Cumbernauld, 25th April 1975.

The inscribed decanter which was
presented to C.M.G. on that occasion
and one of the six glasses inscribed
with one of MacDiarmid's poems
gifted by Michael Grieve to his father
at Christmas 1975.

L

*Photo: Gordon Wright*

Major F. A. C. Boothby and C.M.G. at Brownsbank, 1975.

Major F. A. C. Boothby, editor and publisher of *Sgian Dubh — the Newsletter of the National Movement*, and C.M.G., photographed outside Brownsbank in March 1975, prior to Major Boothby's arrest on 29th March 1975 for alleged conspiracy to import explosives· for the purpose of damaging property in connection with the Army of the Provisional Government of Scotland. The A.P.G. consisted of about eight people from widely divergent backgrounds.

The trial was, in the opinion of many, an attempt by the Government to discredit the Scottish National Movement.

C.M.G. gave evidence at the trial, acting as a character witness on Major Boothby's behalf.

The jury, while finding Major Boothby guilty of one of the eight charges, specifically exonerated him of any intent to endanger life.

Major Boothby was sentenced to three years' imprisonment, of which he served thirteen months before being released on parole.

Senior members of major political parties wrote to the Secretary of State for Scotland urging his release.

*Photo: Gordon Wright*

A corner of C.M.G.'s work room at Brownsbank.

C.M.G. with Gwynfor Evans, M.P.,
President of Plaid Cymru, the
Welsh National Party, 1976.

*Photo: Welsh National Party*

With friends at the Common Riding, Langholm, 1975.

C.M.G. and Sorley MacLean at Brownsbank, February 1977.

*Photos: Gordon Wright*

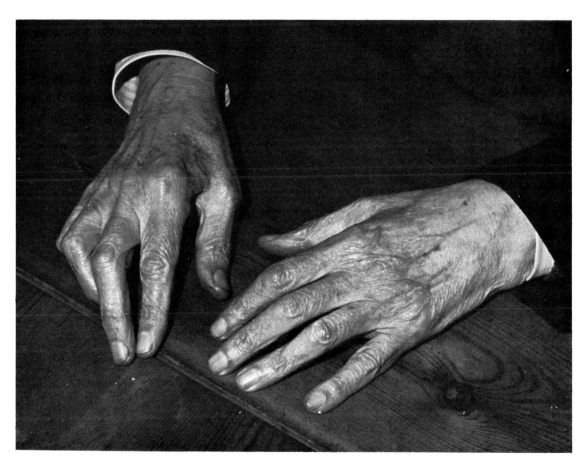

A focus on C.M.G.'s hands as mentioned by Kenneth Buthlay in the introduction. Photo taken 1976.

As Coia sees Hugh MacDiarmid whose epic *A Drunk Man Looks at the Thistle*, written 50 years ago, will be read by Tom Fleming in St Cecilia's Hall tonight. The poet himself will take part in a recital at the Netherbow next Saturday.

*The Scotsman*, Saturday, 4th September 1976.

# CROWDIEKNOWE

Oh to be at Crowdieknowe
When the last trumpet blaws,
An' see the deid come loupin' owre
The auld grey wa's.

Muckle men wi' tousled beards,
I grat at as a bairn
'll scramble frae the croodit clay
Wi' feck o' swearin'.

An' glower at God an' a' his gang
O' angels i' the lift
—Thae trashy bleezin' French-like folk
Wha gar'd them shift!

Fain the weemun-folk'll seek
To mak' them haud their row
—*Fegs, God's no blate gin he stirs up*
*The men o' Crowdieknowe!*

Photo: *Gordon Wright*

C.M.G. at Crowdieknowe graveyard, near Waterbeck, where many of his ancestors are buried.

# CHRONOLOGY

| | |
|---|---|
| 1892 | Born at Arkinholm Terrace, Langholm, 11th August. |
| 1896 | Moved to the house in Henry Street. |
| 1897 | Enrolled in Langholm Infant School. |
| 1899 | Enrolled in the primary department, Langholm Academy. |
| | Moved to the house in Library Buildings. |
| 1904 | Transferred to the secondary department, Langholm Academy. |
| 1905 | Teaching in Sunday school. |
| | Started contributing to the local newspaper. |
| 1908 | Admitted as a pupil teacher to Broughton Higher Grade School and Junior Student Centre, Edinburgh. Joined the Edinburgh Central Branch of the Independent Labour Party of Great Britain and the Edinburgh University branch of the Fabian Society. |
| 1909 | Edited *The Broughton Magazine*, Christmas 1909 to summer 1910. |
| 1910 | Left Broughton and freelanced as a journalist in Langholm. |
| | Worked as a journalist with *Edinburgh Evening Dispatch* for about one year. |
| 1911 | Returned to Langholm to freelance. Father died. Left Scotland for South Wales to work on the *Monmouthshire Labour News*. |
| 1912 | Returned to Langholm. Moved to Clydebank to work on the *Clydebank and Renfrew Press*. Rejoined the Independent Labour Party. Moved to Cupar to work for three associated newspapers. Met Peggy Skinner. |
| 1913 | Moved to Forfar to work on *The Forfar Review*. |
| 1915 | Enlisted. |
| 1916 | Promoted to sergeant. Served with 42nd General Hospital R.A.M.C. in Salonika. Suffered first attack of malaria. |
| 1918 | Invalided home to the Malaria Concentration Centre, North Wales. Married Peggy Skinner. Posted to Sections Lahore Indian General Hospital in France. |
| 1919 | Demobbed. Joined his wife in St Andrews. Found work with *The Montrose Review* and moved to live in Montrose. |
| 1920 | Moved to Kildermorie, E. Ross and Cromarty to teach. |
| 1921 | Returned to work for *The Montrose Review*. |
| 1922 | Settled in at 16 Links Avenue, Montrose. Elected to the town council of Montrose as an Independent Socialist. |
| 1923 | Joined PEN International. |
| 1924 | Peggy gave birth to Christine. |
| 1925 | Applied unsuccessfully for the post of Keeper of the National Gallery of Scotland. |
| 1926 | Appointed Justice of the Peace. |
| 1927 | Founded the Scottish Centre of PEN. |
| 1928 | Founder member of the National Party of Scotland. |
| 1929 | Peggy gave birth to Walter. Moved to London to edit *Vox*. |
| 1930 | Separated from Peggy. Moved to Liverpool to work as a public relations officer. |
| 1931 | Met Valda Trevlyn in London. Delegate to the PEN Congress in Vienna. |
| 1932 | Divorced from Peggy. Moved to Thakeham in Surrey. Valda gave birth to Michael. Returned to Edinburgh. Employed as editor of *The Free Man*. Living in Longniddry. |
| 1933 | Returned to Edinburgh. Moved to the island of Whalsay. Expelled from the National Party of Scotland. Candidate in Aberdeen University Rectorial election. |
| 1934 | Joined the Communist Party of Great Britain. Mother died. Planned to retrieve the Stone of Destiny. |
| 1935 | Candidate in Edinburgh University Rectorial election. Nervous breakdown. |
| 1936 | Candidate in Edinburgh University Rectorial election. |
| 1937 | Expelled from the Communist Party but reinstated on appeal to the National Executive. |
| 1938 | Expelled from the Communist Party for Nationalist deviation. |
| 1941 | Conscripted for National Service. |
| 1942 | Rejoined the Scottish National Party. Member of S.N.P. National Council until 1948. |
| 1943 | Transferred to the Merchant Service as first engineer on H.M.V. *Gurli*. |
| 1945 | Independent Scottish Nationalist candidate for Kelvingrove in the General Election. Registered as unemployed in Glasgow. Brief period as reporter with *The Carlisle Journal*. |
| 1948 | Left the Scottish National Party. |
| 1950 | Visited Russia with members of the Scottish-U.S.S.R. Friendship Society. Moved to Dungavel House, Strathaven. Independent Scottish National Party candidate for Kelvingrove, Glasgow, in the General Election. Received a Civil List pension. |
| 1951 | Moved into Brownsbank Cottage, near Biggar, Lanarkshire. |
| 1956 | Rejoined the Communist Party. Visited China with the British-Chinese Friendship Society. |
| 1957 | Awarded Honorary LL.D. by Edinburgh University. Made honorary member of Scottish PEN. |

| | |
|---|---|
| 1958 | Presented with the Andrew Fletcher of Saltoun Medal for "Service to Scotland" by Edinburgh University Nationalist Club. Candidate in St Andrews University Rectorial election. |
| 1959 | Installed as Club Bard with Sydney Goodsir Smith and Norman MacCaig, at the first supper of the 200 Burns Club. Visited Czechoslovakia, Rumania, Bulgaria and Hungary as part of the Burns bi-centenary celebrations. |
| 1960 | Candidate in Aberdeen University Rectorial election. |
| 1963 | Presented with the William Foyle Poetry Prize for 1962. |
| 1964 | Visited Canada. Communist candidate for Kinross and West Perthshire in the General Election. |
| 1967 | Installed as President of the 1320 Club. Seventy-fifth birthday exhibition in the National Library of Scotland. Visited the U.S.A. |
| 1968 | Elected an Honorary Fellow of the Modern Language Association of America. Awarded £1,000 by the Scottish Arts Council in recognition of his contribution to Scottish literature. |
| 1971 | Visited Italy. Became patron of the 1320 Club on the death of Lord Boyd Orr. |
| 1972 | Eightieth birthday symposium at Edinburgh University. MacDiarmid exhibition in Edinburgh University Library, MacDiarmid exhibition in The People's Palace Museum, Glasgow. Elected President of the newly formed Lallans Society. Created a Governor of the Academy of Pure Malt Scotch Whisky. |
| 1973 | Visited Ireland. Took part in the Rotterdam International Poetry Festival. |
| 1974 | Elected an Honorary Member of the Royal Scottish Academy as Professor of Literature. |
| 1975 | Received the freedom of the Burgh of Cumbernauld. |
| 1976 | Visited Canada. |

# CHECK LIST OF PUBLICATIONS

1909-10   Edited *The Broughton Magazine*.
1920      Edited *Northern Numbers*.
1921      Edited *Northern Numbers*. Second series.
1922      Edited *Northern Numbers*. Third series.
1922-23   Edited *The Scottish Chapbook*.
1923      Edited *The Scottish Nation*.
      *Annals of the Five Senses*.
1924      Edited *The Northern Review*.
1925      *Sangschaw*.
1926      *Penny Wheep*.
      *A Drunk Man Looks at the Thistle*.
      Edited *Robert Burns, 1759-1796*.
      *Contemporary Scottish Studies*. First series.
1927      *Albyn, or Scotland and the Future*.
      *The Lucky Bag*.
      *The Present Position of Scottish Music*.
1928      *The Present Condition of Scottish Arts and Affairs*.
      *The Scottish National Association of April Fools*.
1929      *Scotland in 1980*.
1930      *To Circumjack Cencrastus, or The Curly Snake*.
      *Annals of the Five Senses*, reissued.
1931      Edited *Living Scottish Poets*.
      *First Hymn to Lenin and Other Poems*.
1932      *Second Hymn to Lenin*.
      *Scots Unbound and Other Poems*.
1934      *Five Bits of Miller*.
      *Scottish Scene, or The Intelligent Man's Guide to Albyn* (with Lewis Grassic Gibbon).
      *Stony Limits and Other Poems*.
      *At the Sign of the Thistle*.
      *Selected Poems*.
1935      Translated *Alexander MacDonald: The Birlinn of Clanranald*.
      *Second Hymn to Lenin and Other Poems*.
1936      *Scottish Eccentrics*.
1938      *Scotland and the Question of a Popular Front against Fascism and War*.
      *Dìreadh (I)*.
1938-39   Edited *The Voice of Scotland*.
1939      *The Islands of Scotland*.
1940      Edited *The Golden Treasury of Scottish Poetry*.
1943      *Cornish Heroic Song for Valda Trevlyn*.
      *Lucky Poet: a Self-Study in Literature and Political Ideas*.
1944      *Selected Poems*. Edited by R. Crombie Saunders.
1945-49   Edited *The Voice of Scotland*, revived.
1946      *Speaking for Scotland*.
      *Poems of the East-West Synthesis*.
1947      *A Kist of Whistles: new poems*.
1948      Edited *William Soutar: Collected Poems*.
1949      Edited *Robert Burns: Poems*.
      Edited *Poetry Scotland*. No 4.
1950      Edited *Scottish Art and Letters*. No. 5.
1952      *Cunninghame Graham: a centenary study*.
      *The Politics and Poetry of Hugh MacDiarmid*.
      Edited *Selections from the Poems of William Dunbar*.
1953      *A Drunk Man Looks at the Thistle*. New edition.
1954      *Selected Poems*. Edited by Oliver Brown.
1955      *Francis George Scott: an essay*.
      *In Memoriam James Joyce*.
      Edited *Selected Poems of William Dunbar*.
1955-58   Edited *The Voice of Scotland*, revived again.
1956      *Stony Limits and Scots Unbound and Other Poems*.
      *A Drunk Man Looks at the Thistle*. Third edition.
1957      *Three Hymns to Lenin*.
      *The Battle Continues*.
1959      *Burns Today and Tomorrow*.

| 1961 | *The Kind of Poetry I Want.* |
|------|------------------------------|
|      | *David Hume, Scotland's Greatest Son.* |
| 1962 | *The Man of (Almost) Independent Mind.* |
|      | *Collected Poems.* |
|      | *A Drunk Man Looks at the Thistle.* Fourth edition. |
|      | *The Ugly Birds Without Wings.* |
|      | *When the Rat Race is Over:* an essay. |
|      | Edited *Robert Burns: Love Songs.* |
| 1963 | Adapted *Harry Martinson: Aniara* (with Elspeth Harley Schubert). |
|      | *Sydney Goodsir Smith.* |
|      | *Poems to Paintings by William Johnstone 1933.* |
| 1966 | *The Company I've Kept.* |
| 1967 | *A Lap of Honour.* |
|      | *Collected Poems.* Revised edition. |
| 1968 | *Celtic Nationalism* (with Owen Dudley Edwards, Gwynfor Evans and Ioan Rhys). |
|      | *Early Lyrics.* Edited by J. K. Annand. |
|      | *The Uncanny Scot: a selection of prose.* Edited by Kenneth Buthlay. |
|      | *An Afternoon With Hugh MacDiarmid.* |
| 1969 | *A Clyack-Sheaf.* |
|      | *A Drunk Man Looks at the Thistle.* Illustrated by Frans Masereel. |
|      | *Selected Essays.* Edited by Duncan Glen. |
| 1970 | *More Collected Poems.* |
|      | *The MacDiarmids: a conversation.* |
|      | *Selected Poems.* Edited by David Craig and John Manson. |
| 1971 | *A Drunk Man Looks at the Thistle.* Edited by John C. Weston. |
| 1972 | *The Hugh MacDiarmid Anthology.* Edited by Michael Grieve and Alexander Scott. |
|      | *A Political Speech.* |
|      | *Scottish Eccentrics,* reissued. |
|      | *Lucky-Poet,* reissued. |
| 1973 | *Song of the Seraphim.* |
|      | Edited *Henryson.* |
|      | Translated *Bertolt Brecht: The Threepenny Opera.* |
| 1974 | *Dìreadh I, II and III.* |
|      | *Scottish Scene* (with Lewis Grassic Gibbon), reissued. |
|      | *Scotch Whisky* (with others). |
| 1975 | *Metaphysics and Poetry.* |
| 1976 | *Contemporary Scottish Studies.* Enlarged edition. |
|      | *John Knox* (with Campbell Maclean and Anthony Ross). |

# RECORDS

| 1962 | *The Poetry of Hugh MacDiarmid.* Spoken by Iain Cuthbertson and the author. |
|------|------------------------------------------------------------------------------|
| 1967 | *The Legend and the Man:* readings from Burns and MacDiarmid by Hugh MacDiarmid. |
| 1968 | *Hugh MacDiarmid reads his own Poetry.* |
| 1970 | *A Drunk Man Looks at the Thistle:* Hugh MacDiarmid reads his own poem. |

# INDEX

173

174

175